The GLORY DAYS of BUFFALO SHOPPING

MICHAEL F. RIZZO

THE
History
PRESS

Published by The History Press
Charleston, SC 29403
www.historypress.net

Copyright © 2013 by Michael F. Rizzo
All rights reserved

Cover images, front: AM&A's courtesy of Buffalo State College Archives, Courier-Express
Collection; A&P from author's collection; Sattler's courtesy of the Voorhees family. Back:
A&P from author's collection; Woolworth's courtesy of www.woolworthmuseum.co.uk;
Super Duper courtesy of Ken Goudy.

First published 2013

Manufactured in the United States

ISBN 978.1.62619.301.7

Library of Congress CIP data applied for.

This book is dedicated to my mom,
a lady who instilled confidence in us in her own way.

Contents

Preface

My mother and stepfather were managers and buyers for Consolidated Millinery, which operated the hat and wig department of the downtown AM&A's store until the closing in 1994. Their office was across the street in a small, old, kinda creepy office. There was a super creepy tunnel that went under the street to the building and an old freight elevator. It was so cool. I was in my early twenties and worked for the fine jewelry office, which was also incredibly small, but loved the job. I will always remember AM&A's and still have them on my résumé to this day!

—anonymous

This book isn't going to answer every question about why Buffalo's great shopping destinations closed. Whether it was the Seneca Mall or Adam, Meldrum & Anderson (AM&A's), Hengerer's or Sattler's, they all had a similar ending. Downtown Buffalo experienced major construction in the late 1970s with the rapid transit that tore up Main Street right through the heart of the shopping district and probably sealed the fate of some of the stores already teetering on the edge of survival.

There were three shopping centers I remember visiting when I was younger: Southgate Plaza and Seneca Mall in West Seneca and Thruway Mall in Cheektowaga. My most vivid memory of Southgate was in the 1970s, when it had an Acme grocery store. At one point, Acme had a collectible hockey stamp book and released new stamps to add to the book. My mother would drive me there every week to collect the new stamps until I eventually filled the book, and unlike my G.I. Joe with the "kung fu grip," I still have the book.

I remember going to Seneca Mall after school and seeing the fancy Sattler's store. At the time, I had no understanding of what Sattler's used to be, but I remember the huge letters on the wall. Lastly, Thruway Mall was nearing the end of its life when I started going there. I remember walking through the mall in the late 1980s and seeing a few Buffalo Bills players sitting at a table to sign autographs, but there was no one in line. It was before the team began its rise to fame and Super Bowl years. It was sad to see—kind of like the mall itself at the time, right before the Walden Galleria opened and sucked the life from it.

But just when *were* the "glory days" of Buffalo shopping? It seems that time frame is from about the 1940s through the 1970s. Almost anyone over a certain age knows what 998 is. Or a Pup Sale. Or a blue light special. Or the Bargain Train. These are part of retailing history.

In 1950, the Cold War was on, but Buffalo mayor Joseph Mruk was beaming, as his city of Buffalo, New York, had a population of 580,000, with no end in sight. The city was alive both day and night with workers, shopping, a thriving theater district and plenty of traffic. Main Street had more than two hundred stores, restaurants, theaters, banks and radio studios, as well as a post office. There were bowling alleys, taverns, hotels, offices and railroad terminals.

Fast-forward to 1978. Urban renewal had dramatically changed downtown, with the elimination of thousands of residents and the construction of the Main Place Mall, which replaced perfectly good commercial structures. The light-rail rapid transit construction began on Main Street, and the six-year construction project subsequently banned vehicle traffic from Tupper Street to Church Street in order to create a pedestrian mall, a popular design idea at the time.

The prolonged construction and street closing were definitely factors in the decline of retailing and the golden age of shopping in downtown. But these were only part of the reason. The true reasons for the decline vary, but much of it started when the local mom and pop stores were pushed out of business by the larger chain stores or were gobbled up by them through expansion. There were many other factors at work, including changing demographics, recessions and unemployment.

The soldiers returning from World War II also made a tremendous impact throughout the 1950s. Many of them chose not to live in the cities where they grew up but rather moved to the suburbs to buy new houses in new developments with their U.S. Department of Veterans Affairs (VA) loans. You can't blame them, but these families moving out of the city had a long-lasting effect on Buffalo's decline. Shopping plazas and malls started to pop up around these new housing developments to accommodate the new suburban dwellers. Many of Buffalo's stores, once located just downtown or in the Broadway-Fillmore neighborhood, started to open branches in these new plazas and malls, stretching their resources and diminishing their value while slowly giving shoppers reasons not to visit downtown or Broadway-Fillmore.

One point that resonates throughout this book is how the fate of many local businesses came under the axe of out-of-town owners, people who didn't understand the city or the people and looked at everything in purely financial terms. The real problem, though, was that poor business decisions often played a large part in so many of those outcomes. The same mistakes were made over and over. A conglomerate buys dozens of companies, grows too fast and then experiences a recession or is overburdened with debt payments, so stores need to be closed or they file bankruptcy. It's just numbers. No one cares what happens to the hundreds of employees who needed those jobs.

"Sure, it's hard to close these stores," stated Harvey A. Weinberg, "but remember, I sliced away 100 before I left Hartmarx."[1] Weinberg was president and chief executive of HSSA Group Ltd., the company that bought and eventually closed Kleinhans clothing store. It was just a numbers game to him.

Miami Herald columnist Leonard Pitts Jr. summed up the impact local stores had on our lives best in a February 1, 2006 column: "They gave the neighborhood personality. They gave it soul."[2]

Soul, and the unique characteristics of our stores, is what we remember, what we feel in our hearts: the cheap dresses at Gutman's, the way you were greeted at Kleinhans, the variety at Barnum's, the Hellzapoppin' Sattler's sales and the semiannual "Pup" Sales at the Sample. The stores all had soul; they were part of the community. The founders poured their lives, their blood and their souls into those buildings, those stores, and gave them life. We shopped there because it was Buffalo, because they understood us. And when their existence ended, a part of us died too.

The purpose of this book is to explore the wonderful stores that once graced the shopping districts of Buffalo. This book has a lot of information but still barely scratches the surface. As a result, the book is not meant to be a comprehensive list of every store in Buffalo but rather a broad overview.

Main Street in downtown Buffalo was the department store and apparel center of the area, and the Broadway-Fillmore neighborhood became the discount store area. Other business districts that were important but are not explored in the book include Grant-Ferry, Kensington-Bailey, Elmwood-Hertel, Jefferson-Utica and Seneca Street.

One thing I find very interesting is what the value or cost of something one hundred years ago equates to in today's dollars. So, after many of the dollar values, you will see a different number in parentheses. That number is the current value as of 2010, which I extracted from the website measuringworth.com. It gives you a better idea of what $100,000 in 1910 means in today's dollars. You will be amazed at how much money the stores spent on remodeling as they grew, or how much sales they were making.

This book could not have been completed without the help of many people and places. As always, the Buffalo and Erie County Public Library Central Branch Grosvenor Room's excellent local history collection and wonderful staff were extremely helpful. Most of the research and many photos were found there. Thanks also to Daniel Dilardo, archivist at Buffalo State College, and special thanks to Peter Cammarata and Jack Hahn for their insight in the first edition. Thanks to the many corporations that allowed use of their logos. Thanks to John and Mary Neumann for the great Sattler's photo. Thanks to Martin Biniasz; Bob Sinkiewicz; Mitch Gerber; Michael Miller; Derrick Clements, archivist, Weston Corporate Archives; Barbara A. Campagna; Mary Ann Voorhees; Marcie and Marvin Frankel; Donna Petrillo; and David Bunis for additional photos and/or family history. Thanks, too, to Paul Seaton and woolworthsmuseum.co.uk. Also, I couldn't have completed this without the Internet and fultonhistory.org.

Thanks, as always, to my wife, Michelle, who sits back while I immerse myself in my work. As a revision to an earlier work, there was less to do the second time around, but as I searched for new photos, I spent many hours online.

We can't bring the stores back, but we can remember their soul, the happy memories they invoke and the sadness we felt when they closed. And we can love them. I loved just writing about them, and it brought back many memories. Since the first edition was released in 2007, I have done many talks and met hundreds of people who fondly remember the stores, their trips downtown or to Broadway with their parents, shopping on Main Street, the AM&A's Christmas displays, tearooms and many other wonderful memories.

I hope this book brings back many memories for you, too. I look forward to your comments about the book and the stores and to your recollections.

Introduction

My first memories of shopping were in Sattler's. My dad would drive us to go shopping on Saturday. He'd leave us at the information station and tell us he'd meet us at a given time. Later, when I graduated from high school, my first job was at Sattler's. There I met my best friend and later, my husband. And yes, I still have the same husband. That is why it's sad to see it in this picture. I have so many, many great memories that are attached to this building. It has to be one of my favorite places in the world.

—anonymous

Although 1816 is seen as the year Buffalo, New York, became a village, and though 1832 was the year it was incorporated as a city, Buffalo was really born in 1825. That was the year the Erie Canal officially opened, with Buffalo at the western terminus. Goods could now be channeled from the east to the west and west to the east, with Buffalo at the midpoint.

All types of trade could now be made, from grain to cloth, hardware and leather. The animal stockyards in Buffalo quickly grew, only to be surpassed by Chicago years later. This provided outlets for leather goods as well as foodstuffs. With the goods flowing and the population increasing, it became advantageous to open food markets, general stores, wholesale and retail. Retailing quickly began to flourish as this small village grew into a city. Some of the earliest stores include Weed, Flint & Kent and the forerunners to Hengerer's and Stewart & Benson, all of which opened before 1850 and all of which survived into the twentieth century.

According to 1948 census figures, downtown accounted for 24 percent of all retail sales in Erie County, with the rest of Buffalo accounting for an additional 54 percent, meaning that 78 percent of all sales in Erie County originated in Buffalo! Keep in mind that this was shortly after World War II ended, and the exodus to the suburbs was just beginning, with 61 percent of the population still residing in Buffalo.[3]

The total purchases downtown amounted to what would equal more than $1.62 billion in today's dollars, accounting for 58 percent of general merchandise and 62 percent of all apparel purchases in the county. Lovejoy, which included the Broadway-Fillmore district, accounted for the second-largest buying area, amounting to $803 million in today's dollars.

As you can see, retailing was big business in Buffalo, and as it moved to the suburbs with the people, it would forever change the way people shopped, where they spent their money and the reason many had for coming into the city.

Chain Stores

I am frequently asked the reasons for chain store success. There are many reasons,
but they can all be boiled down to this: KNOWLEDGE.[4]
—department store founder William. T. Grant

Buffalo's location has always been attractive to national firms. Whether it was an appliance chain, a clothing chain or a department store chain, Buffalo has had a fair share of stores come and go over the years. Some were so beloved that sometimes you didn't even know they weren't locally owned.

Most of the large chains had stores in Buffalo in the early part of the twentieth century, including Sears, Lerner and Kresge. According to Godfrey M. Lebhar in his 1963 book *Chain Stores in America*, Woolworth, Kresge, A&P, J.C. Penney, Sears and others experienced phenomenal growth up until about 1930. At that time, they started to catch their breath and organize their growth. Then the Depression hit. When they were ready to begin expanding again, World War II broke out and civilian construction was banned, and there were also merchandise and manpower shortages. Many of the companies began building larger stores, so they needed fewer stores; in the case of A&P, it closed several thousand stores.

The discount department stores—such as King's, Two Guys, Twin Fair and others—grew in a similar manner. Most formed from the 1950s through the 1960s, expanding in the 1970s and finally ending with financial and operational failures in the 1980s. Two Guys grew by recycling stores closed by bankrupt chains. "[The year] 1982 marked a peak in the demise of discounters," with at least four closing, including Twin Fair locally. Three filed Chapter 11 and eventually closed, including King's.[5]

When a local store, such as AM&A's, was purchased by a nonlocal company, the public generally felt that the end was near. With AM&A's, the name change to the Bon-Ton Stores Inc. spelled the end of the city's best-loved department store. But when it closed the downtown headquarters, it was the end of retailing on Main Street as we knew it.

When Chicago's famous Marshall Field's department store was changed to Macy's in September 2006, there were more than one hundred demonstrators who protested the name change. At the same time, hundreds of curious shoppers waited outside the store entrance two hours before it opened to see the new store.

Chain stores have always gone to where the people and money are, whether it is Starbucks opening next to a local coffee shop or an appliance chain opening up with a huge marketing campaign. Many factors have contributed to the change in the Buffalo retailing climate. Some can be attributed to the chain store, and some have been Buffalo's lack of planning and the lack of community leaders in the second half of the twentieth century.

KOBACKER'S

The first H. Kobacker's Sons store (of Columbus, Ohio) to open in Buffalo was in 1921, at 1018–1028 Broadway, in the former Siegrist & Fraley furniture store. It added a store at Broadway-Fillmore when Eckhardt's closed its store, running it under the Boston Store brand.

Kobacker's extended its reach to downtown Buffalo when it purchased Baker's department store at 392–394 Main Street in May 1938, keeping former owner Alexander Weiss on as manager. Baker's had been open since 1925 and had operated the store after taking over the building that Walbridge & Company had vacated for its new building on Court Street.

In 1950, Kobacker's opened a store at 827 Tonawanda Street, purchasing the former Rowland's Department Store. A $500,000 expansion was made to the Broadway store in 1954, adding a three-story building and another floor to the original structure. Renovations to the other local locations and the opening of a store in the Northtown Plaza in 1955 and the Southgate Plaza in October 1957 continued the local growth.

In 1961, the chain merged with Davidson Bros. Inc., which operated Federal Department Stores. In 1963, it closed the Broadway store after a forty-two-year run. The company announced plans to become the first new department store built in downtown in about thirty years in 1966, when it would anchor the new Main Place Mall. "The store will be a $1.75 million [$11.8 million] reflection of our faith in Buffalo," stated Joseph Ross, president of Davidson Bros. Inc.

By 1972, the outlook of Federal's Inc., the new name of the company, had changed, and it filed for Chapter 11 bankruptcy protection. In September 1972, the Northtown Plaza and Tonawanda Street stores were shuttered, and in December 1972, the company closed the downtown and Southgate Plaza stores, along with other stores in the chain, in order to concentrate on its core in Detroit and Flint, Michigan.

This was a common ending to many Buffalo stores when they were sold to out-of-town interests.

Year opened in Buffalo: 1921
Year closed: 1972

KRESGE, KMART, NEISNER AND BIG N

S.S. Kresge Inc. was started in 1899 in Detroit, Michigan, as a typical five-and-ten store by Sebastian S. Kresge. By the time it incorporated in 1912, it was operating eighty-five stores.[6] In 1920, the first Buffalo listing for Kresge's is at 388 and 472 Main Street. It quickly expanded in Buffalo, adding stores on Grant and Tonawanda Streets and Delaware Avenue by 1930. Its stores were larger and carried more merchandise than the typical five-and-ten, which was a precursor to the modern discount department store.[7]

By 1950, it had nine city locations, but that number had dwindled to four by 1960. In 1962, the company opened its first Kmart discount department store in Michigan, which meant the eventual death of Kresge as a store. In 1966, it planned three Buffalo-area stores, but by 1977, the company had been renamed K-Mart Corporation. The Main Street store was closed before 1970, but the Grant Street and Central Park Plaza locations held on longer. In 1987, it sold the last of its Kresge stores,[8] and in 2005, the struggling Kmart merged with Sears.

S.S. Kresge was a popular competitor to Woolworth's. It opened many stores across Buffalo, including on Grant Street. This logo still survives on that store. *Photo by author.*

Neisner Brothers Inc. was a five-and-ten chain based in Rochester, New York. Its first Buffalo store opened at 965 Broadway in 1923. It was slow to open additional locations, adding Broadway-Fillmore and Bailey Avenue locations by 1935. In 1938, it opened a new flagship store that it built at 460 Main Street, and by 1950, there were several suburban locations. By 1966, there were at least twelve Neisner's stores locally.[9] Many people remember the wooden floor in the store and the "blue light specials" (special in-store sales). People also fondly recall the cafeteria in the basement.

Valu Discount Department Stores Inc. was based in Niagara Falls, New York, and opened a store in the Rossler Plaza in Cheektowaga in 1967.[10] Neisner's, apparently following the Kmart model, opened Big N, a discount department store, when it purchased the Valu store in 1969.[11]

It opened additional stores in the area until December 1977, when it filed for Chapter 11 bankruptcy protection.[12] In January 1978, it announced the closing of all of its stores,[13] and by November 1978, it had been purchased by Ames, which converted most of the Big N stores to Ames sites.[14] As of 1980, the Broadway location of Neisner Brothers Inc. was still open, but it was no longer listed in 1982.

In the mid-2000s, the façade of its long-empty Main Street store was removed during remodeling to reveal the former clock that once adorned the front of the store.

TWO GUYS

Two Guys was started in 1946 by brothers Herb and Sid Hubschman, who ran a snack counter in the RCA building in Harrison, New Jersey. The brothers came across scratched televisions one day in the factory and made a deal with RCA to sell them. They put fliers out in the neighborhood and sold all the televisions in a few hours. RCA continued supplying the scratched and dented items, and the brothers became legends. News of their prices infuriated other local appliance dealers, and they became known as "those two bastards from Harrison."[15]

When it came time to incorporate, they almost kept the name "Two Bastards from Harrison," but they realized that no one would run their ads, so the name was changed to Two Guys from Harrison. The "from Harrison" part of the name was eventually dropped, and it was soon just called Two Guys. The brothers were leaders in the fight against blue laws (designed to enforce moral standards, particularly the observance of stores being closed on Sundays).[16] The company grew by purchasing bankrupt stores.

In 1959, the chain acquired the O.A. Sutton Company, makers of the Vornado line of fans, and became Vornado Inc.[17] At that time, it was operating just fourteen stores, but by 1970, the company had two Buffalo-area stores and, at its peak, had more than one hundred stores across upstate New York and other areas. In late 1980, it was acquired by Interstate Department Stores, which began liquidating the stores. In 1981, it closed thirty-two stores as Vornado began exiting the retail trade. In February 1982, Vornado said that it had closed its last twelve stores as part of a plan to become a real estate development company, prompted by an inability to halt continuing losses.[18] At least one local plaza is still owned by Vornado.

Two Guys was a discount department store chain from New Jersey started by two brothers selling bruised RCA televisions. They had several local stores. This was an ad from their going-out-of-business sale. *Author's collection.*

17

King's was another discount department store chain started in Massachusetts. It had four locations in the Buffalo area by the mid-1970s. This was a Christmas ad in the local newspaper. *Author's collection.*

KING'S

King's Department Stores Inc. was started in Brockton, Massachusetts, in 1956. As of 1970, it had 2 local stores, eventually adding 1 more suburban location. It was interested in some of the closing W.T. Grant stores in 1976 but later withdrew its bids.[19] The company had about 190 stores when it purchased the bankrupt Mammoth Mart chain in 1978, which operated primarily in New England.[20] This debt eventually forced King's to file Chapter 11 bankruptcy protection in 1982 and to close all its stores in 1984. Ames purchased the chain and reopened many of the stores as Ames sites.

Gold Circle, Hills and Ames

Gold Circle was an upscale discount department store chain, similar to Target, owned by Lazarus Department Stores and founded in 1968. It was later owned by Federated Department Stores Inc.

Gold Circle first opened in the Buffalo area in the 1970s. The stores were popular, but in 1986, its parent company merged two divisions it owned, finally closing all the Gold Circle stores in 1988. Hills Department Stores purchased thirty-nine former Gold Circle stores, including several in Buffalo.

In 1979, Buffalo first welcomed Hills Department Stores of Canton, Massachusetts. The discount chain was started in 1957 by founder Herbert H. Goldberger, one of the first retailers to believe in "everyday low prices." The company kept prices down by not accepting credit cards.[21]

It built new stores and was in competition with Two Guys, Kmart, Twin Fair and Ames. In November 1981, it opened its seventh local store. In 1991, the chain filed for Chapter 11 bankruptcy protection, eventually emerging, with 30 percent fewer stores, in 1993.

Ames's entry into the Buffalo market also happened in the 1970s. The company was started in Southbridge, Massachusetts, with the concept of opening in small and rural towns in the Northeast,[22] much like Walmart. It purchased the stores of many bankrupt chains, which allowed it to expand rapidly.

Saddled with debt from poor business decisions, the company filed for Chapter 11 bankruptcy protection in 1990, emerging from bankruptcy in 1992 and returning to profitability. As Walmart began opening stores in the Buffalo area, Ames began closing stores in proximity, mainly in the rural communities that both Walmart and Ames served.

In 1998, Hills was acquired by rival Ames, creating the fourth-largest discount retailer in the country. But Ames apparently didn't learn from its previous poor business decisions, and in 2001, it sought Chapter 11 bankruptcy protection for a second time. Again saddled with enormous debt and unable to fix the massive problems it brought on, it announced in August 2002 the closing of all 452 stores in the chain. Many local stores are still empty.

HUDSON'S

The year 1881 was a special one in Detroit, Michigan, as that was the year Joseph L. Hudson opened his first J.L. Hudson department store, forever changing the way people shopped in that city and in others.

In 1886, Hudson made a trip to Buffalo and opened a specialty branch at 392 and 394 Main Street, concentrating on men's and boys' wear. Hudson's younger brother, William, moved to Buffalo in 1896 and took over local operations as vice-president. In 1899, they moved to 410 Main Street.

Joseph Hudson was the major investor in the Hudson Motor Car Company in 1909 and died in 1912. The stores continued to grow until there were a total of fifteen. In 1928, William Hudson died, having been president of the Hudson Company for fifteen years. He left an estate valued at $1 million ($12.7 million) and was returned to Detroit for burial.

A few years later, in 1932, Robert B. Adam of Adam, Meldrum & Anderson Company announced the purchase of the Buffalo store, which adjoined the AM&A's store on Main Street. The sale was reported at $350,000 ($5.59 million). AM&A's continued to operate the store as a separate menswear branch, but by 1946, it had abandoned the Hudson name to concentrate on the AM&A's brand.

The store was closed in 1960 when AM&A's closed its own store to move across the street,

The J.L. Hudson men's clothing store was started in Detroit. It opened a location on Main Street in Buffalo in 1886 that was later sold to AM&A's. Hudson was the major investor in the Hudson Motor Car Company. *Author's collection.*

and all the buildings up to its store were demolished for construction of the Main Place Mall.

The Hudson flagship store in Detroit contained thirty-three levels and was the tallest department store building in the country. When the City of Detroit decided to demolish the building in the late 1990s, there was public outcry, but the city prevailed. It was the largest building ever imploded.[23]

Tearooms were restaurants located in stores geared toward female shoppers. Oppenheim, Collins was an upscale ladies' clothing store from New York City that opened a Buffalo branch in 1905. Miss Vincent's Tea Room was very popular after a long day of shopping. *Author's collection.*

Oppenheim, Collins & Company

Not every store of memory was locally born and bred. This particular store saw potential in Buffalo long before many others found their way here. In 1905, New York City–based Oppenheim, Collins & Company Inc. opened a branch at 534 Main Street in Buffalo. Known as an upscale women's clothing store, it became popular among Buffalonians who wanted high-quality fashion and full service.

At the time of the store's opening, Buffalo was a rising star among cities, with a rapidly growing population, many wealthy citizens and a fast-growing retail district. The store took five of seven stories in the building it occupied and was remodeled several times over the years. In 1929, it took over the top two floors and extensively remodeled the building, adding "an elaborate beauty parlor…and the building of a fur storage plant on the seventh floor."[24] As did many stores of the time, Oppenheim, Collins had a restaurant on the premises—in its case Miss Vincent's Tea Room, where between "the hours of 11 A.M. to 3 P.M.," an express elevator only ran to the Tea Room.

The store was again remodeled in 1935 and 1951. At the time of the 1949 announcement of the remodeling, the president of the firm stated, "[W]e are very much sold on suburban operations."[25] This was shortly after World War II had ended, and the numbers moving to the suburbs were increasing exponentially. It wasn't until 1956 that it opened that branch, and it was at the Thruway Plaza.

Oppenheim, Collins diversified over the years, adding children's and juniors' departments. In 1951, it added a "modern candy department,"[26] and in later years, it added Top of the Town restaurant.

Franklin Simon was another New York clothing retailer that started in 1902 and had multiple branches in several states. In 1962, the two chains were merged, and all the stores were re-branded as Franklin Simon Company. By 1979, the parent company of Franklin Simon had closed all forty stores in the chain.

The Buffalo store at 534 Main Street was taken over by Holly Shop for a short time.

A&P

The Great Atlantic & Pacific Tea Company (A&P) was founded in Elmira, New York, in 1859. By 1876, it had sixty-seven stores, opening the first Buffalo location in 1898. By 1925, there were ninety-six branches in the Buffalo area alone.

A&P was an innovator in many ways. It was the first grocery store chain to reach one hundred stores and the first "supermarket," each with an in-store bakery.[27] By the 1930s, the chain had sixteen thousand stores, grossing more than $1 billion ($13.1 billion) annually.[28] It created *Woman's Day* magazine in 1931, sold exclusively through its stores, and was a pioneer of in-house brands, such as Eight O'Clock Coffee, Jane Parker and Ann Page foods. The brands were so popular that many people didn't realize they were in-house brands.

The Great Atlantic & Pacific Tea Company, better known as A&P, grew to be a large grocery chain. It opened a Buffalo warehouse on Hamburg Street in about 1925 that supplied hundreds of stores. Its store brands, like Eight O'Clock Coffee, became nationally known. *Author's collection.*

By 1925, A&P had a local warehouse at 519 Hamburg Street that would end up supplying more than five hundred stores.[29] The warehouse stored produce and groceries, and on the third floor of the building, "coffee from South and Central America is blended into A&P's own three famous brands—Red Circle, 8 O'clock and Bokar." It also had a modern egg handling plant and a bakery that mixed and packaged "bread, cake, pies, doughnuts, cookies and other baked goods."[30]

Many of the small mom and pop A&Ps eventually gave way to supermarkets. In the 1940s, the company began operating larger A&P Food Stores supermarkets and reduced the number of stores in Buffalo to 27. By 1958, the company had eclipsed its nearest competitor by $1 billion in sales, and A&P became the leading grocery chain in the United States. But by the 1960s, A&P had competition from the larger suburban stores in Buffalo and around the country. Its once popular house brands were losing favor as "national television advertising drives increas[ed] customer demand

Above: The Great Atlantic & Pacific Tea Company produced thousands of ads over the years. It was a powerhouse in Buffalo, and this magazine ad is from 1945. *Author's collection.*

Opposite: A&P constructed a factory on Hamburg Street in Buffalo to supply hundreds of stores. The building is still standing, and the logo is still very visible. *Photo by author.*

for national brand products."[31] There were 20 stores in Buffalo in 1960. The company struggled to survive over the decade and closed 2,885 stores nationwide; it was down to just 15 in Buffalo by 1970.

The changing tide was too much, and senior management was unable to right the ship. So, in March 1970, the company announced that it was closing the Buffalo bakery, which supplied eighty stores. On April 10, 1975, the company announced that it was pulling out of the Buffalo market completely.[32] Other local chains were interested in the stores, including S.M. Flickinger Company, which purchased some of the closing A&P stores and converted them into its Super Duper brand. In 1978, Flickinger again bid on closing A&P stores, this time in Ohio.

In 1979, the company was sold to the Tengelmann Group of West Germany. The company began purchasing small grocery chains and working to reconfigure itself. Although a much smaller company compared to its peak in the 1930s, A&P, under its various brands, operates three hundred stores in the Northeast in 2013.[33]

W.T. Grant

In 1906, William T. Grant opened his first W.T. Grant store in Massachusetts. The store was known as a twenty-five-cent store, a little pricier than the standard five-and-dime.[34] The concept was successful, and Grant began opening stores at a record pace. In 1922, he opened his first Buffalo location at 546–552 Main Street. The store was popular, and the company saw even more potential in the Buffalo market, so it purchased adjoining property to build a larger store in 1928. The sale price of more than $13 million in today's dollars was quite astonishing and said to be a record price for Main Street real estate at the time.[35]

With the onset of the Depression and other factors, the new store wasn't built until 1939, at which time it was the largest store in the chain. The building cost $7 million in today's dollars and was of an extremely modern design. Its curved façade is one of the things often remembered about the building. Founder William T. Grant was on hand for the ribbon cutting for what would become the most profitable store in the chain for many years.[36]

In 1941, the company opened a store in the University Plaza, adding to its other four stores locally. In 1966, it expanded its Main Street store, taking over the first floor of the former Flint & Kent store at 560 Main Street,[37] adjacent to its building.

Grant's (as it was known) was slow to realize the potential of the suburb, and unlike its peer, Kresge, which opened Kmart in the early 1960s,[38] the first local "Grant City" department store didn't open until 1966, on Main Street and Transit Road in Clarence.[39] The stores were not of uniform design and size and were not nearly as popular.

By 1975, the chain was on life support, partly due to bad business decisions, such as paying stockholder dividends even when the company was losing money. On February 14, 1976, an unhappy Valentine's Day, all twenty-four stores in the Buffalo area were closed, with six reopening for a short time as clearance centers. Ames purchased two local stores, and King's had placed bids on three stores but withdrew them.

The grand downtown store that was so modern in 1939 was demolished in 1981 to make room for the new headquarters of Liberty National Bank, which was owned by Norstar Bank. As the Norstar site was being readied for the new bank, the foundations of three prior buildings, including Grant's, were found there. This led to added costs for removal of the foundations, as

W.T. Grant started as a twenty-five-cent store. At one point, it had nine local stores, but mismanagement at the headquarters doomed the chain, and in 1976, it experienced the second-largest bankruptcy in United States history and went out of business. *Author's collection.*

there was no space left for the new foundations. However, a benefit of earlier times was given to the site, as along Huron Street there was a sidewalk grate of sizeable proportion, left over from the days when coal was dumped into the building basement. Such "rooms" under the sidewalk became natural locations for "electrical vaults" that need ventilation.[40]

Today, the site is part of Fountain Plaza.

E.W. EDWARDS & SON

The story of E.W. Edwards & Son began in Johnstown, New York, in 1832. Growing from one dry goods store, it moved to Syracuse and opened a second store and then a third in Rochester. The continued success drove it to the burgeoning Buffalo market in 1922.[41]

It was at that time that H.A. Meldrum Company, at 460 Main Street, was bankrupt, so E.W. Edwards took advantage of the situation and purchased the assets of the company and leased its building. The purchase price was $451,000 ($5.86 million), and Daniel M. Edwards moved to Buffalo to run the local store.

In 1925, the company purchased the Lockwood building on Franklin Street and the old Star Theater, which was demolished in 1924, as well as other property adjoining it at Mohawk, Pearl, Genesee and Franklin Streets, to build "one of the largest and most completely equipped department stores in New York state."[42]

The new store was opened on September 13, 1926, with 82,900 square feet of floor space and was connected to two other buildings that the store already occupied. Plate glass covered 10,000 square feet of the new building, and the first floor was dedicated just to furniture. The store was said to have one of the largest tunnels in the state, connecting the basement of 460 Main Street, under Pearl Street, to the new store on Pearl Street.[43]

Edward L. Hengerer, son of William Hengerer, was made president of the firm in 1934 after Daniel Edwards died, after having worked for Hengerer's and Lord & Taylor. Financial woes struck the company— probably the reason Hengerer was brought in since he had performed a turnaround for Lord & Taylor—and under his leadership, profits increased.

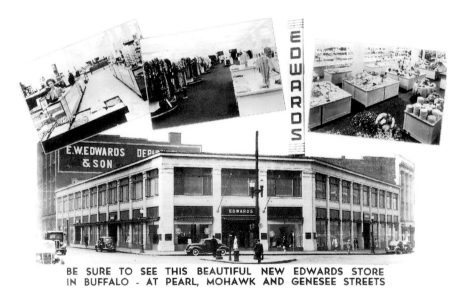

BE SURE TO SEE THIS BEAUTIFUL NEW EDWARDS STORE IN BUFFALO - AT PEARL, MOHAWK AND GENESEE STREETS

E.W. Edwards & Son built a beautiful new store downtown in 1926. This postcard shows the store from several angles after its opening. *Courtesy of Russ Grasso.*

In May 1938, the Edwards store ended its run at 460 Main Street when its lease expired. The company planned an expansion of some of the property it already owned, opening a new store that same month,[44] with thirty thousand to forty thousand Buffalonians attending the grand opening. It took over the Mohican Market at 155–157 Franklin Street and moved its appliance department there.[45]

Business did well, and it expanded the Buffalo store, acquiring more property and opening additional departments, with new additions and remodeling done throughout the 1940s.[46]

Experiencing a sales slump due to World War II, the company embarked "on a program of bringing prices down to where the public again can afford to buy items it needs."[47] Macy's in New York City had made the same change the previous week, and locally, Sattler's and Hens & Kelly admitted to the same practice.

E.W. Edwards & Son announced a small five-thousand-square-foot store for Bailey Avenue in the Langfield Plaza in June 1947. This store was designed to "serve a sufficiently large segment of the population of Buffalo to warrant establishing a branch in this area."[48] The store was successful, and in 1950, it quadrupled the store size. The company was "convinced there is a definite need for suburban shopping centers"[49] and opened a branch in the L.B. Smith Plaza in Lackawanna in October 1951.[50]

Business seemed to be doing well, but the financial woes it had experienced twenty years earlier resurfaced. "E.W. Edwards & Son announced plans to terminate its merchandising operation in the city of Buffalo, New York as of December 31, 1952," and to concentrate on its Syracuse and Rochester stores.[51] "The management…wishes to thank the employees of the Buffalo store for their loyal and diligent service to the company and to thank the many thousands of customers who have, over the years, favored E.W. Edwards & Son with their patronage."[52]

AM&A's took over the L.B. Smith Plaza location, and Hens & Kelly took over the Langfield Plaza store.[53]

OTHER CHAINS

The New York Lerner Company (later Lerner Shops Inc.) opened a new $100,000 store at 504–506 Main Street in July 1937, having been on Main Street since 1930. The store stuck through the many changes downtown, later moving into the Main Place Mall for a time and later exiting the city for its suburban stores.

"The nation's largest clothing chain,"[54] Robert Hall Clothes, came bursting into the Buffalo market in 1954, opening 5 stores. The 162-store chain opened 1 store in the city at 5 Kensington Avenue and the rest in the suburbs. The chain grew to 430 stores and was a profit producer for its parent firm. When losses started to mount in the 1970s, due to "stores predominantly located in urban centers and the lack of enough stores in the increasingly popular suburban shopping malls,"[55] the company decided to shut them all down. In June 1977, they were all closed—with the assets being purchased by International Fastener Research Corporation, the same company that had dismantled Weed & Company in 1963—and sold as individual units.[56]

At one time, there were many small grocery chains throughout the area. Mohican Markets operated seven Buffalo-area stores. This is a newspaper ad from the era. *Author's collection.*

The Mohican Company operated a chain of grocery stores located in Connecticut, New York City, Lockport and Buffalo, with other cities likely. Sometime in about 1930, the company opened three Mohican Markets in Buffalo, and in 1937, the company opened a new market, offices and a warehouse on Main Street near Fillmore Avenue. "The building is an expression of our belief in the future of the Main-Fillmore community."[57] By 1940, there were eight branches; by 1960, there were three; and by 1965, there were none. Several of the locations became Bells IGA Markets.

Norbans women's clothing store is another name that many may remember. Founded by Joseph Norban in about 1938, its first listing was at 620 Main Street, and by 1940, it was listed at 479–481 Main Street. The

Norbans was a ladies' clothing store that grew to thirteen locations. This location was a "self-service" department store located downtown. Eventually expanding to eighty-five stores, it filed for bankruptcy in 1988. *Courtesy of David Torke.*

chain apparently franchised its operation and expanded rapidly locally, with 3188 Bailey Avenue, 1549 Genesee Street, 66 Grant Street and 1328 Jefferson Avenue all open by 1950. In 1960, it became Norbans Self Service Department Store, with additional locations at 832 Tonawanda Street, 667 Main Street (today a youth hostel), 690 Fillmore Avenue and 2172 Seneca Street, and three of the original locations had moved to presumably larger stores on Grant, Jefferson and Bailey. By 1964, there were five additional locations, for a total of thirteen. By 1987, it was down to just four locations: Main, Grant, Broadway and Bailey. In 1988, Joe Norban Inc. filed for bankruptcy, shuttering eighty-five stores it had open in the Northeast and Midwest. Although a photo exists of a location on Washington and Huron Streets, a listing for one could not be found.

McCrory's was a national chain of five-and-dime stores started in Pennsylvania. One early investor was Sebastian S. Kresge, who operated his own chain and later traded stores with McCrory. The firm had 6 locations locally, plus 3 under the G.C. Murphy name. In 1999, it opened in the shuttered F.W. Woolworth store at 395 Main Street, a welcome addition after the surprise closing of the downtown store. The company had weathered some storms, emerging from bankruptcy in 1997 as a smaller operation and re-branding 3 Buffalo stores as

Dollar Zone. But in 2001, it was down to 193 stores, from a high of 1,300, and closed those remaining in February 2001.

C.A. Weed & Company was a clothing manufacturing concern from Binghamton, New York. In early 1901, it opened a store in Buffalo at 416–418 Main Street. After less than two years, it had outgrown the building and contracted with local architects Green & Wicks to design a new building. The foundation for the new store, which was seven stories high, had "eight folds of steel beams—the largest ever cast in Buffalo."[58] The men's and boys' furnishing store was open until 1921.

J.C. Penney opened its first store in Buffalo in 1940, opening a store outside all the big retail areas at 2883 Bailey near Kensington Avenues. It left the Buffalo area just a few short years later, only to return in 1952 and open a store at the new Thruway Plaza.

Another chain store was Interstate Department Stores (IDS), which was a draw at the Central Park Plaza and had several suburban locations. In 1978, it went bankrupt and emerged as Toys "R" Us.

Sears, one of America's first department store chains and one of the largest, came to Buffalo back in 1928. It was such a big affair that Mayor Frank Schwab held a press conference as he and executives from Sears signed the deed transferring the former Carnival Court Amusement Park property on Main Street and Jefferson Avenue to Sears.

The store opened in 1929, and the company grew rapidly, opening a store at 2220 Seneca Street in 1938, adding a $300,000 addition to the Main Street store and a store at 950 Broadway in 1949, building a $1 million ($9.14 million) warehouse in 1954 and opening a store in the Thruway Plaza in 1957.

It closed the Broadway store in 1957 and began opening more suburban stores, including a $5 million store at the Southgate Plaza in 1959, "the largest shopping-center store leased by Sears east of the Mississippi River."[59] In 1968, it donated land on Main Street to Canisius College, and in 1980, it announced the closing of its original Buffalo store at 1905 Main Street. Reasons included shoplifting and changing demographics. The store had originally served a large area, but many new stores covering the area made it less necessary to keep this store open.

Blue Cross of Buffalo used the remodeled store for its headquarters for many years and in the 2000s sold it to Canisius College.

Discount Stores

I worked at National Gypsum on Delaware next to the Chez Ami and remember changing from our high heels to race to Main Street to shop at all the stores.[60]
—a downtown lady shopper

The five-and-dime, five-and-ten or whatever name it went by was a phenomenon unlike any other. The rise of these stores played out in cities all over the country. Woolworth's, S.H. Knox & Company, Neisner Brothers, Kresge, Kress, J.J. Newberry, G.C. Murphy and W.T. Grant are some of the best-known examples. Many of these chains started in New York, Pennsylvania and the Midwest, so Buffalo was in a prime location and was a testing ground or expansion location for many of them.

Locally, we had our own pioneer five-and-dime store, S.H. Knox & Company, as well as local stores. The five-and-dime store and the department store each had its own niche. The five-and-dime sold inexpensive variety goods, had a smaller store layout and usually had a lunch counter. The department store was usually bigger, carried more expensive items and had a restaurant.

Then came the discount department store. S.S. Kresge was an early developer, opening Kmart, as was Neisner's with its Big N. Locally, Twin Fair was one of the only chains, but we had our fair share of regional and national chains, such as Two Guys, King's, IDS, Gold Circle, Hills and Ames. Later on, Walmart and Target would enter the Buffalo market, and it would never be the same.

Most of the discount department stores did not have locations in the city of Buffalo. By the time they opened locations in Western New York, the suburbs were

The predecessor to Woolworth's was opened in Reading, Pennsylvania, by cousins Seymour H. Knox and Frank W. Woolworth in 1898. This was the store at the beginning. *Courtesy of www.woolworthsmuseum.co.uk.*

the fertile ground for expansion. Kmart, Gold Circle, Hills and Twin Fair had city locations. After mergers, Gold Circle and Ames had city locations. In later years, after most of the department stores had closed, Target opened city locations.

S.H. Knox and F.W. Woolworth

The Knox family name in Buffalo is not as prevalent as it once was, but many years ago, it evoked power and prestige, as the family was involved in cultural and community events. It all started when Seymour H. Knox traveled to Reading, Pennsylvania, with his cousin, Frank W. Woolworth, to start a five-and-ten store,[61] where the price of everything was either five or ten cents. The "stock generally consists of everything from a needle to a threshing machine, but threshing machines have dropped out of fashion [in 1898]."[62]

The concept, although not completely new, was perfected by the cousins, and "young Knox soon sold out his interest in the Reading store and decided to establish another of the same kind in Newark."[63] This store was just as successful, and Knox eventually sold out and went to Erie, Pennsylvania, to join his cousin in Woolworth & Knox, another store. The pair found the formula that worked, and in about 1888, Knox went to Buffalo to open another store at 409 Main Street. That was followed by another in Lockport, New York, the following year.[64] The Erie partnership was dissolved, with Woolworth continuing that operation alone.

Shortly after starting the Buffalo store, Knox bought out Woolworth's share in the store and established S.H. Knox & Company, with headquarters in Buffalo. He continued expanding his new chain, opening stores in Detroit, Toledo and Lowell, Massachusetts, as well as many more cities. He added a store at 520 William Street in Buffalo and opened what is said to be the first Canadian five-and-ten in Toronto.[65]

The Main Street store, located in the Wonderland Building, was destroyed in a December 1893 fire, so it moved to 395 Main Street. "When the Mooney-Brisbane building was completed [on the site of the Wonderland Building], Mr. Knox rented one of the largest stores, and the rental of it, together with the others, exceeds $40,000 [$1 million] a year."[66]

The "syndicate," as it was called, was run from offices in the Prudential Building, with a "corps" of stenographers. The Brisbane store employed about fifty with the goal to get customers in and out as quickly as possible.

The customer would be waited on immediately upon entering the store, "and in less than five minutes after is on his or her way out again."[67]

S.H. Knox & Company was a very successful operation, growing to 112 stores, all run from headquarters in Buffalo. This allowed Mr. Knox to accumulate great wealth, but even that would be surpassed in the near future.

In 1912, a meeting of Woolworth; his cousin, Knox; and four others, all owners of five-and-ten stores, resulted in the merging of their companies to form the F.W. Woolworth Company. Woolworth had the largest share, followed by Knox, who became vice-president of the new company. The Buffalo offices became head of the Buffalo division of the Woolworth company. By 1915, the company had eight hundred stores in the United States and Canada and fifty in England.[68]

In 1939, the Buffalo Brisbane store building's size was doubled with the addition of a basement sales floor.[69] The Woolworth company continued to grow and "eventually incorporated lunch counters and served as general gathering places, a precursor to the modern shopping mall food court."[70]

The company built the tallest building in the world in 1913 in New York City, and even though competitors pressured it, it continued to be the dominant five-and-ten store. In the 1960s, the five-and-ten gave way to a larger format, the discount department store, with Kresge opening Kmart, Neisner's opening

The merger of Seymour Knox's 112 five-and-ten stores with F.W. Woolworth and three others created the greatest discount chain store in the world. This is the Brisbane Building store on Main Street in Buffalo in the late 1970s. *Courtesy of Buffalo State College Archives,* Courier-Express *Collection.*

Big N and Woolworth opening Woolco in 1962. Coincidentally, this was the same year the first Target and Walmart opened.[71]

The company had expanded by opening or purchasing other chains, including Kinney Shoes and Foot Locker. In 1983, it closed the Woolco chain, and by 1997, competition had driven it down to just four hundred Woolworth stores.

On July 17, 1997, the company announced that it was closing the remaining Woolworth stores. "The post war exodus to the suburbs soon created pressures, as shoppers left behind Woolworth's and other Main Street stores for malls and larger stores on high-ways."[72] The company hadn't followed its customers and lost many of them. The company changed its name to Venator and focused on its other brands. In 2001, it changed its name again to Foot Locker Inc.[73]

The accumulated wealth had allowed Seymour Knox to collect a great number of art works, many of which were donated to the Albright Art Gallery. He bred and raced horses and owned a large farm in East Aurora, New York (today Knox Farm State Park). He built a mansion at 1024 Delaware Avenue and was chairman of the board of Marine National Bank and a director at several others over the years.

His son and grandsons played important roles in Buffalo, including sponsoring an addition to the Albright Art Gallery and as founders of the Buffalo Sabres hockey organization, among many other endeavors.

Year opened: 1888
Year closed: 1997

TWIN FAIR

In the 1950s, the retail landscape was changing as the suburbs became the home for returning World War II vets, and many retailers followed. On March 22, 1956, the Twin Fair Inc. was incorporated by John J. Bona, Anthony Ragusa, Louis Battaglia and John J. Nasca. The plan was to operate in a new forum known as discount merchandising, which was a relatively new concept at the time. Twin Fair "began with one store on Walden Avenue, well out of the high rent district."[74] With the exception of Nasca, the founders were "all experienced merchandisers."[75]

The first store, smaller than the later Walden Avenue store, proved profitable, so the founders continued to open stores. By 1959, they had four stores, and

Twin Fair was a local discount department store chain that grew to 8 stores. After the merger with a larger company, it grew to 375 stores in the 1970s and purchased the struggling Hens & Kelly chain in 1978. By 1982, it was down to 14 stores that were sold, many former Twin Fair stores becoming Gold Circle. *Author's collection.*

sales were $2.5 million ($18.7 million) annually as they embarked on an expansion at all four stores and planned two new ones. "We are convinced that the growth potentials for the Niagara Frontier fully justify all this expansion," stated company president John J. Nasca in November 1959.[76]

"They had Buffalo virtually surrounded with a chain of six,"[77] but "the fast expansion had thinned the owners' working capital."[78] Hence, to keep costs down, they leased departments to outside interests. The company still retained control of merchandising, advertising and other operations, but this allowed it to concentrate on business growth.

In March 1962, the founders sold their interests to Unexcelled Chemical Corporation, which was a diversified company operating varied businesses. The company continued its local growth under the new ownership, opening three more stores, including a city branch on East Ferry Street. It added credit and supermarkets in half its stores. The food concept started in 1962 when it needed to fill a "35,000 square foot expansion of the Niagara Falls Boulevard store."

Twin Fair's profits continued to grow as CPA Harold Egan took over as president under Unexcelled. In three years, he increased sales from $10 million to $22 million ($157 million), increased its advertising and "expanded and upgraded merchandise lines."[79] The success of Twin Fair and other similar companies of its time proved to manufacturers that profits could still be made through discounters, especially "in hard goods and food." Clothing manufacturers still were less receptive to the concept in 1965. "Discounters who have not succeeded have failed, Egan believes, because of careless business practices. Poor financial planning leading to over expansion, Egan says, frequently has been the key to the discounter's failure."[80]

The company had plans to open a new warehouse, a downtown store and "two or three additional stores throughout Buffalo"[81] and also employed more than one thousand people in 1965. It opened its eighth local store on Seneca Street in Buffalo in 1967. In May, it opened a liquor store adjacent to the Walden Avenue store. It purchased a Cincinnati chain of stores in 1968 and in 1969 merged a Connecticut corporation into Twin Fair.

In 1970, it formed Twin Fair Distributors Corporation to operate its chain stores, and by then, it had built a chain of 375 stores concentrated in New York and Ohio. In 1978, it purchased the struggling local department store chain Hens & Kelly. The addition was supposed to be the crown jewel in its portfolio, but several years later, the purchase was draining its bank account.

The once popular Twin Fair chain was down to just fourteen stores by 1982, all in the Western New York area, where it had originated. The saving grace came when Federated Department Stores Inc. purchased the remaining stores, leaving Twin Fair Inc. to continue operations "as a real estate holding and development concern."[82]

In return, Twin Fair received a $2.5 million loan, and Federated reopened the Twin Fair stores as Gold Circle, one of its subsidiaries. On April 13, 1985, Twin Fair Distribution Corporation was terminated, effectively closing the Twin Fair chapter.

In early 1988, Federated was purchased by Campeau Corporation, the Gold Circle chain was sold and many branches became Hills Department Stores.[83]

Year opened: 1956
Year closed: 1982

Clothing and Jewelry Stores

I would rather lose a sale than lose a customer.
—Buffalo jeweler Harry Gamler

It has long been said that clothes make the man. Years ago, men and women would dress up whenever they went out of the house, wearing hats, suits and dresses everywhere—and not sideways ball caps but fedoras and other conventional hats. Men also dressed in suits and ties much more often. A trip to go shopping downtown usually meant wearing your Sunday best.

Clothing can make a person feel like they are on top of the world, and Buffalo had its fair share of clothing stores, such as Kleinhans, the Sample, L.L. Berger and many small stores that came and went. Buffalo was full of clothing factories, leather factories, shoe stores and stores that sold just hats or coats. You could get any type of clothing you wanted, and it was probably made right in Buffalo. If not, it may have been a European import. As times changed, the chain stores and several recessions eventually forced many of the local companies out of business.

The Sample and L.L. Berger were facing so many of the same dire consequences in the late 1980s that they actually talked about merging. But apparently, circumstances prevented the actual merging, which might have been enough to save two of Buffalo's famous stores if it had actually happened.

The 1970s weren't especially kind to Kleinhans either. Several new chains threatened its hold on the men's clothing market. The stodgy upscale shopping experience wasn't for everyone, and when Syms moved onto Main

Street, Kleinhans must have felt the heat. Mantwo was another discount store that opened in the Bailey-Kensington area at about the same time. Together, they probably contributed to the decline in Kleinhans with their self-service style and off-price merchandise.

With the shopping mall experience and chain jewelry outlets, stores like Gamlers became less of a necessity.

CRESBURY CLOTHES

The history of this company runs through several generations, a number of companies and multiple locations. In about 1915, Samuel Seeberg opened a clothing store at 1092 Broadway at the corner of Loepere Street. His sons, Edward and Harry, along with their six other siblings, all worked there.

In 1926, Harry and Edward opened their own store, at 340 Washington Street, after Edward returned from college. According to one story, the brothers split up in 1936, with Harry starting H. Seeberg Inc. and Edward joining with Samuel David to open Seton's at 355 Main Street. According to the 1930 city directory, though, Harry already was in business.

In 1939, Edward Seeberg and Samuel David were able to purchase Crescent Creations, a clothing manufacturer located at 50 Exchange Street. They also purchased Ray's Clothes in Niagara Falls, which they continued to operate as a separate entity. At some point, the company's name was changed to Cresbury Clothes Inc. In 1948, it opened its first Cresbury branch at 891 Broadway, and two years later, it opened a store in Jamestown, New York. Those stores were eventually closed as the company "decided to concentrate on locating stores in the expanding Buffalo suburbs."[84]

It purchased land near major plazas and opened standalone stores. The first of these stores was in 1953 at 3600 Delaware Avenue in the town of Tonawanda, followed by 1530 Walden Avenue across from Thruway Plaza in Cheektowaga in 1959.

In 1959, Seeberg formed a union with Richman Brothers to develop a national chain of men's clothing stores, although nothing was planned for the Buffalo area. Richman Brothers had been in Buffalo going back to the 333 Main Street location in the 1920s.

In 1965, the company opened a new Cresbury branch downtown at 410 Main Street (the former J.L. Hudson store, which closed in 1960 after AM&A's

The Cresbury Company grew to operate seven clothing stores and two factories in the Western New York area. This is a 1970s newspaper ad. *Author's collection.*

moved across the street) since it had to vacate its 355 Main Street location for the construction of the Manufacturers & Traders Trust Company (M&T) office building. In 1970, its manufacturing plant at 50 Exchange Street was torn down as part of the Marine Midland bank office tower construction, and in 1976, it celebrated its fiftieth anniversary.

By 1980, there were only three stores left, and in 1982, it closed two, leaving only the Walden Avenue store. Edward Seeberg announced the closing of the last store in May 1983 so he could concentrate on his real estate interests, ending the life of Cresbury's.

Year founded: 1936
Year closed: 1983

DIXIE HAT SHOP

William Kaufman and David Gross were involved in the millinery business (a business that designs, makes, trims or sells women's hats) dating back to 1935. Gross was manager of Siegel's, a woman's furnishings store located at 532 Main Street, and Kaufman was manager of Palace Millinery at 477 Washington Street. Siegel's was owned by Max Siegel, who operated as an importer dating to 1925. In 1936, Jackson Millinery Inc. was formed. Kaufman opened Dixie Sample Hat Shop in Utica, New York, that same year. He and Gross opened a location in downtown Buffalo in 1937 at Washington and Eagle Streets, where hats sold for $1.25.[85]

By 1946, Gross and Kaufman were both involved in Jackson Millinery Company Inc., first located at 630 High Street and then, by 1950, at 138 Grant Street as "milliners."[86] In 1955, Dixie's Hats Inc. was incorporated in Ohio, and it added locations at 585 Main Street, 1331 Jefferson Avenue and 22 Court Street.

Dixie's, as it was often called, was one of the first local businesses to show filmed television commercials.[87] Additional locations were opened as the company grew, including in Lockport, Niagara Falls and Kenmore, and by 1965, it had closed its original Grant Street location. In 1970, there was a Dixie's Hats Inc. located at 1233 Main Street, third floor, along with Dixie's Sample Hat Shop on Court Street and a location in the new Main Place Mall.

Dixie's Hats grew to have two dozen stores in three states. Many Buffalo ladies purchased inexpensive hats and gloves at its stores and have fond memories of the experience. It advertised hats at "$1.99, $2.99, $3.99; none higher."

David Gross and William Kaufman both retired in 1971 and sold the company to the parent company of Claire's Boutiques. In 1973, Dixie's Hats and Barbara Dale Inc. of Pennsylvania were merged into Jackson Millinery. Gross died in 2001 and Kaufman in 2004. Both lived into their nineties.

Year founded: 1950
Year closed: 1971

GUTMAN'S

Gutman's was a popular women's clothing chain started in 1947 by Alvin H. Gutman. The first location was at 584 Main Street, and in 1955, it added a branch at 91 Grant Street. By 1960, it had added one at 959 Broadway.

The local chain, known for spectacular sales, was very successful in Buffalo and was able to duplicate that success, at one point operating twenty-eight stores in several states.[88] Locally, the company felt that malls were the future, eventually moving its Main Street store into the Main Place Mall when that opened in the mid-1960s. Other locations included five suburban malls.

In 1985, the company filed for Chapter 11 reorganization, with debts eating away at the company. At the time, it was down to seventeen stores in New York, Michigan, Ohio and Virginia. In 1989, it closed its Seneca Mall location, which had lost all its major tenants to the McKinley and Galleria Malls and was failing. The following year, it opened an off-price outlet in the Thruway Mall (formerly Plaza), which was losing the battle with the Walden Galleria a mile away.

In June 1991, it closed the Galleria, McKinley and Main Place Mall stores. The Galleria store was located near two other local stores

Gutman's was a popular Buffalo women's clothing chain. This is a typical newspaper advertisement from the company.

at the mall that had recently closed, Sample and L.L. Berger, leaving less of a draw for Gutman's. Together with cash flow problems, thinly stocked stores and losses mounting, it filed for Chapter 11 bankruptcy protection again in July 1991.

Following a troubled summer, it shuttered all of its locations in August 1991 except the Eastern Hills Mall.

Year founded: 1947
Year closed: 1991

THE JACOBI BROTHERS

The Jacobi name is still well known as a seller of quality menswear, even though it hasn't been around for years. In 1919, Martin, Norman and Frank Jacobi opened their first Jacobi Brothers store at 2163 Seneca Street, near Cazenovia Parkway, not far from their South Buffalo home. In 1924, the store moved downtown to 734 Main Street, and in 1936, it moved to a new location at 628 Main Street.

The Jacobi brothers all ran men's clothing stores in Buffalo. Martin Jacobi set off on his own to run Martin Jacobi Inc. This newspaper ad was from 1934. *Author's collection.*

The exterior of Martin Jacobi's store at 599 Main Street in Buffalo during a bleak time in downtown history. *Courtesy of David Torke.*

A 1926 news article about Martin, the oldest at thirty, quoted him as saying, "All for one, one for all, and all for Buffalo!"[89] That apparently changed because in 1932, Martin opened his own store at 599 Main Street. Business prospered, and in 1944, he purchased the building at 618–620 Main Street and announced plans to establish "one of the finest men's clothing stores in this section of the country" after the end of World War II.[90] The new building featured Greek columns and a modern interior design and was finally occupied in 1949.

By 1946, Jacobi Brothers had moved to 505 Main Street. It opened a branch in the Thruway Plaza, and in 1957, it had a location at 2313 Harlem Road. By 1973, the brothers had left downtown for their suburban stores. In 1984, Jacobi Brothers added a location at 4545 Transit Road, and by 1991, the company had closed its last location on Transit.

Martin Jacobi continued to ride out the storm downtown through the rapid transit construction, which was the final blow to many Main Street businesses. Unfortunately, time took its toll, and between 1981 and 1982, the store was closed.

Year founded: 1919
Year Martin Jacobi closed: 1982
Year Jacobi Bros. closed: 1991

THE KLEINHANS COMPANY

In 1880, Edward L. Kleinhans left his hometown of Pontiac, Michigan, to work in his brother Horace's clothing store in Louisville, Kentucky. His hard work paid off, and he was enticed to run a clothing store in Chicago.

In 1893, he and his brother traveled to Buffalo and opened the H. Kleinhans & Company clothing store at 259 Main Street. When the Mooney-Brisbane building was erected at Main, Washington and Clinton Streets and opened in 1896, the fast-growing company took over two floors in the new building.

Unfortunately, Kleinhans went bankrupt in March 1902, and Herman Rosenberg of Rochester purchased and sold the stock of the store. He must have liked Edward Kleinhans because the company was incorporated as the Kleinhans Company on March 4, 1902, with Herman Rosenberg the controlling shareholder; Edward Rosenberg and Edward Kleinhans were the other minority shareholders, with Kleinhans holding one single share of stock. Horace Kleinhans died in 1903.

When the Kleinhans brothers started their company, they were so sure of the quality of their products that they guaranteed every purchase or refunded the customer's money. By 1923, Edward Kleinhans had rebuilt the business and regained control of the company (with the majority stake of 3,900 shares of stock) and was president, while Edward Rosenberg had a minority stake and was

Kleinhans had a tough time in its early years, eventually going bankrupt. Through hard work, Edward Kleinhans was able to right the ship and left a fortune to establish Kleinhans Music Hall in Buffalo. This was an early newspaper ad. *Author's collection.*

secretary of the company. In early 1934, Kleinhans died, followed four months later by his wife. He left an estate valued at $817,476 ($11.9 million), plus the sale of his personal belongings, to establish a music hall to be given to the city. In 1940, the world-class Kleinhans Music Hall was opened to the public.

John Steurenagel took over day-to-day operations of the company upon Edward's death and continued with the company until 1964. When the company closed in 1992, it was said that Steurenagel had guided the company through even greater success than Kleinhans had.

In 1938, local architects Bley & Lyman designed updates to the store, including new doors, display windows and a pink granite façade. This was in addition to the 1937 updates of air conditioning, an Italian mosaic floor and terra-cotta dome in the second-floor clothing section.

The business continued to grow and was said to be the largest men's clothing store in the country, with fifty-four thousand square feet of selling space, including the basement and two floors in the renamed Brisbane building.

It proudly claimed that "nine out of every ten prominent Buffalonians have a Kleinhans charge account." The company had a fleet of delivery trucks covering ninety thousand miles per year and took care of its employees with profit sharing and full retirement packages, all paid for by the company.

By 1967, the company was in negotiations to be sold, with several suitors apparently interested, until clothing manufacturer and retailer Hart, Schaffner & Marx of Chicago purchased the company in late 1967. At that time, the corporate name was changed to Kleinhart Clothing Inc.

In 1983, Hart, Schaffner & Marx changed its name to Hartmarx Inc. and also took local control away from Kleinhans, as well as most of the other stores it owned. From 1983 to 1988, Kleinhans was said to be the most profitable store group in that division. By 1990, though, there was a recession, a changing buying public, more casual dress in the business world and financial problems at Hartmarx, including a 73 percent drop in profits in 1989, so something had to give.

Kleinhans appeared to be doing well, and it opened a store in the McKinley Mall and closed the Seneca Mall store, but Kleinhans management had been slow to change with the times. Hartmarx began closing stores to try and regain profitability in its Specialty Stores division, which included Kleinhans.

The Eastern Hills Mall store was closed in 1992 after the lease expired. In July of that year, Hartmarx announced that its chairman and CEO, Harvey A. Weinberg, was being replaced, and the company closed more stores.

At one point in its growth, Kleinhans was one of the largest men's clothing stores in the country, with fifty thousand square feet over three floors at its flagship Brisbane Building store. *Courtesy of Buffalo State College Archives,* Courier-Express *Collection.*

Then it sold the entire Specialty Stores division to HSSA Group Ltd. In an interesting move, HSSA chose Harvey Weinberg as its CEO and announced that only one-third of the stores it had bought would be kept open.

Six days later, the news came. "Kleinhans fell victim to a retail slump that was exacerbated by the lingering recession and huge losses at the other retail chains that Hartmarx owned."[91] Arun K. Jain, marketing professor at the University at Buffalo, said that "there were better choices available and at better prices."[92] The customers stopped coming, and "Kleinhans failed to keep up with changes in the marketplace."

About a week later, HSSA stated that it would close 100 of the 187 stores it had bought from Hartmarx. Harvey A. Weinberg, president of the company, was not concerned. "Sure, it's hard to close these stores, but remember, I sliced away 100 before I left Hartmarx."[93]

On December 30, 1992, the downtown Buffalo store closed forever, leaving just the Boulevard and Walden Galleria Mall stores open until their shelves were bare.

On February 17, 1993, the company auctioned off anything that was left from its warehouse at 525 Hertel Avenue. Everything from display racks to vintage sewing machines, antiques and company photo albums from a happier time—when retailing in Buffalo was something special and a company picnic was more than just a photo album to be bought at a garage sale.

Year founded: 1893
Year closed: 1992

L.L. BERGER

Louis L. Berger opened his first women's clothing store in Toledo, Ohio, in 1902 with his brother-in-law, Isaac S. Given. After several years, they came to Buffalo to "open a coat and suit shop. Given wanted a store that catered to popular tastes and Berger wanted to sell finer quality merchandise to the 'society' ladies."

After a short time, "they split up, dividing everything in the store...even the spools of thread!"[94] Given's opened up at 452 Main Street, and Berger opened L.L. Berger Inc. at 500 Main Street on May 10, 1905, "devoted to wearing-apparel of the finer type."[95]

Berger aimed to create ready-to-wear clothing for less than custom-made. "From the outset, fashion and quality is our goal and our problem. We are not a department store. The first several years were a nightmare."[96] The store occupied the first floor of the building, expanding as business increased until 1917, when "the store occupied the entire five floors of the present building."[97]

In February 1928, Berger announced a ninety-nine-year lease on the Stewart estate building at 514–518 Main Street, for a total rent of more than $8 million, not including inflation.[98] The building had been home to the A. Victor & Company furniture store, which was moving down the block to its own new building.

The new store opened for business on February 4, 1929, "a new temple of fashion—stately, elegant, beautiful—as glorious in its garb as the glories contained within its high, white walls, that is the new Berger's," exalted the *Courier-Express*.[99] Thousands passed through the front doors of the remodeled store, entering a "wide portal set in the Italian Renaissance building."[100] Expanded product lines included juniors', millinery and shoes.

The founder of L.L. Berger, Lou Berger, posing at his desk for a 1960 newspaper article. *Courtesy of Marcia and Marvin Frankel.*

"Perhaps the most unusual things about the new Berger store at 514 Main Street…is the fact that it is in reality a collection of specialty shops under one roof." It was able to weather the storm of the Great Depression and continued to grow until the onset of World War II, when it began a new expansion.

"It was after much thought and serious consideration that we decided to open the new Berger shop," stated Lou Berger in September 1942, departing from his original concept. "We wanted to carry more casual clothes for morning-to-night activity. We opened the new store at 508 Main Street, just two dozen steps from our present location." The new store was called Casual Shop[101] and added four floors of selling space to the company. "Where only six floors heretofore served, ten will now be at the disposal of milady for fashions and values."[102]

In June 1944, Berger Properties Inc. purchased the YWCA at 19 West Mohawk Street for future development.[103] In January 1945, it purchased 512 Main Street, located between the Casual Shop and the main store. It had

L.L. Berger grew to be one of Buffalo's largest retailers. Selling primarily ladies' clothing, this was its flagship store on Main Street in downtown Buffalo. You can see three different buildings that were connected to form the store. *Courtesy of Buffalo State College Archives,* Courier-Express *Collection.*

been owned by Isaac Given's widow.[104] "In 1944 bridges were constructed linking the third and fourth floors of the two shops,"[105] and it used the YWCA building as a warehouse. It now owned three adjacent buildings and worked to link them together.

The completion of the joining of the three buildings was delayed (until May 1949) when the United States entered World War II. "The problem of uniting these structures into a single entity required much engineering work and a great deal of heavy steel construction."[106] The exterior design was done by Duane Lyman & Associates of Buffalo. The addition allowed for several new and expanded departments to be added.

In August 1953, the company opened its first branch store in the Thruway Plaza. Understanding that the population was changing, Louis L. Berger justified the new store by saying, "Our object in opening the new store is to bring a metropolitan store in the suburbs, where women can shop informally without dressing up and going downtown."

Berger's, as it was often called, was part of a buying office called Specialty Stores Association in New York City. All the stores were family-owned in cities across the country. For many years, buyers went annually to Europe to buy high-style and high-quality leather goods, jewelry and other finery desired by its clientele.[107] Paris had always been where the buyers of women's wear looked for the newest fashions, but Lou Berger felt that by 1953, "American fashions are quickly replacing the old emphasis on Paris."[108]

In 1954, Berger's son, Maxon, who began working in the store in 1935 as a supervisor, took over as president of the firm.[109] The next store it planned to open was in Niagara Falls in 1955, but that didn't materialize. Instead, it purchased 504–506 Main Street, which was occupied by Lerner Shops. The lease expired in 1957, and construction began in January 1958 to link all of its properties together at a cost of about $750,000 ($5.65 million).[110] It opened its second suburban location in the Sheridan Plaza in Town of Tonawanda in July 1960.[111]

In April 1962, it took down the YWCA building. This was also the year Manufacturers & Traders Trust Company tore down the East Side of Main Street between Division and Eagle Streets and Erie County Savings Bank tore down the west side of Main Street at Division Street, both for their new headquarters. George Newbury, president of M&T, said, "I would also strongly suggest the entire block on the East Side of Main Street between North and South Division Streets be cleared out."[112] And it was.

Berger's founder, Louis, died in 1967 at eighty-seven years old. In his obituary, it is mentioned that Berger's was "compared in fashion retailing with Saks Fifth Avenue and Lord & Taylor in New York, I. Magnin in Los Angeles and Neiman Marcus in Dallas."[113]

The following year would prove to be an important one in the company's history. Lou Berger Jr. and his brother-in-law, Gordon Rashman Sr., "agreed to buy out three other members rather than sell the company to out-of-towners."[114] It was the catalyst that would lead to the company's demise.

In 1968, Maxon Berger retired as president due to health concerns, and Louis Berger Jr. took over the reins. Louis started with the company after returning from World War II. He took over as president when his brother resigned and became chairman in 1984.[115]

It opened Spotlight Shoe Shop in its original store at 500 Main Street in 1968. After a $100,000 remodeling was completed, the street-level shop included a movie stage where silent movies were shown occasionally.[116] The chain opened its first mall store in 1969 when it built in the Seneca Mall, followed in July 1970 in the Northtown Plaza. "The Northtown shop will mark the turning point in the design of all future large new suburban stores," said Berger. It opened additional stores in Lockport Mall (1975), at

510 Elmwood Avenue in Buffalo, in Transitown Plaza (1982), in McKinley Mall and in Walden Galleria Mall.

In Berger's last ten years, Louis Jr. was chairman, Gordon Rashman Jr. ("Billy") was president and Marvin Frankel (Gordon Rashman's son-in-law) was executive vice-president. Gloria Berger, Louis Jr.'s wife, was critical in creating and upholding Berger's image for more than twenty years.[117]

Berger was bullish on the future of downtown as a retailing location. "I look at five years, seven years from now with the rapid transit, and with the theater district…Downtown will continue to be our flagship. I just hope there is further development around.[118] And who knows—maybe the future of Berger's is going beyond Buffalo."[119]

While many of Berger's peers were closing during the 1980s, Berger was able to hold steady, at least to the outside world. By 1990, Buffalo's struggling economy, as well as the savings and loan crisis, was taking its toll on the chain. It tried to sell its flagship store, hoping to lease back two floors,[120] but it failed; the chain continued to struggle.

After the 1990 Christmas season, the end began. "Berger's, like many small independent retail clothing chains across the country, has been confronted with fearsome competition, the Middle East crisis and the recession."[121] Because of loans, high credit and tax obligations, the company was unable to "provide its customers with the selection of merchandise" they had expected the previous Christmas season,[122] and sales reflected such.

On January 14, 1991, L.L. Berger filed Chapter 11 for bankruptcy protection,[123] and Lou Berger said that he wasn't sure if the company could survive. In late January, it closed the Lockport Mall and Elmwood Avenue stores. That wasn't enough, and on February 5, 1991, it announced that the chain was going out of business.

"Some of the blame must go to the management," stated Arun K. Jain, University at Buffalo professor of marketing. "I don't know where they fit into the marketplace anymore. Berger's had an image problem…people didn't know what it was."[124]

Louis Berger Jr. shouldered part of the blame for the demise of the chain. He was a big downtown booster who consistently refused to close the flagship store until it was losing $300,000 per year. He held out too long, and it ended up bringing down his whole chain. "I'm one who hung on with downtown too long because I'm too much in love with downtown," he said.[125] "We also made some errors in judgment. We had done well at Northtown [Plaza] from 1970 to 1980, and we felt we could do as well at Transitown Plaza. But we had made a site selection error, and the store…

was too big.[126] My main weakness was a lack of understanding of the financial details of the company."[127]

The downtown store "was much too big, yearly energy costs alone totaled $160,000 even though much of the space was vacant or used for storage." Additionally, the Hyatt construction next door and the rapid transit construction were factors that stopped shoppers from visiting the Main Street store. When the *Courier-Express* closed in 1982, affluent morning readers were lost, plus with only one major newspaper in Buffalo, the advertising rates skyrocketed, which further distanced Berger's from its customers. Berger's was losing money for six years before it closed, and without the deep pockets of its chain store competitors, this eventually caught up with it.

In the end, Lou Berger said that "the 1968 decision by two of the five Berger families in the firm to buy out the other three," which left them "highly leveraged and under capitalized," was probably the turning point and the basis for their decline.[128]

Gordon Rashman Sr. retired in 1983 and died in 1991. Billy Rashman died in 1994.[129] Lou Berger began teaching, and his flagship store sat empty for ten years. He died in February 2002, and his once glamorous store was reborn as upscale apartments and commercial space.

Buffalonians continue to talk about what a first-class store Berger's was and how they miss it. Such stores are rare anywhere today. One special memory is of white-gloved elevator operators carrying well-dressed shoppers to Berger's eight Main Street floors of elegant fashion.[130]

Year founded: 1905
Year closed: 1991

LEOUS AND PALANKER FURRIERS

Eugene M. Leous started Leous Furriers Inc. in 1897, his first location being at 633 Main Street. He is incorrectly listed in the city directory as Eugene "Leons" for several years. Eventually, his three sons—Thomas, Eugene and Alfred—took over the successful furrier business. It was located at 212 Franklin in the early 1930s, and in 1939, it opened up a new store at 650 Main Street.

The company designed and sold all kinds of furs and provided on-site storage "in burglar, insect and fireproof vaults."[131] "The business has become famous for designs and original styles."[132]

In 1934, Joseph Palanker, a Russian immigrant, started his fur business, Joseph Palanker and Sons Inc., at 80 Genesee Street. Like Leous, his business grew and was successful, and his sons, Marvin and Bernard, eventually joined him.

The Leous sons decided to retire simultaneously and sold their business to Palanker in 1968.[133] The company was positioned to continue in its downtown location until the land it was located on was purchased to build the new Buffalo Convention Center. So, in 1976, the company moved to where the money was: Main Street in Williamsville, New York.

In 2000, the company was sold to longtime employee Russell Rizzo. Russell started with the company as the elevator boy at eighteen years old. The company was renamed Furs by Russell Inc.

Year founded: 1897
Year closed: Still active

SAMPLE SHOP

Anne W. Bunis signed the business certificate for Sample Dress Shop at 1635 Hertel Avenue on July 13, 1928, having opened the store the previous year.[134]

Mrs. Bunis and her husband, Louis, had moved to the United States from Russia in 1905 and then to Buffalo in 1927. Anne decided to start a dress shop in her home "because of the success of a home shirt waist and skirt shop she knew of in Rochester."[135]

After a successful buying trip to New York City, where she purchased forty-eight "sample" (one-of-a-kind) dresses, she opened the door to her living room on Hertel Avenue. At first, just her friends and neighbors came by. But word spread of the great $12.75 dresses, and "soon the whole first floor of the house," about five hundred square feet, was crowded with racks and shelves.

Opposite: With business booming, Anne Bunis was able to hire her husband, Lou, to help run their growing Sample company on Hertel Avenue. This is a newspaper ad for one of its popular sales. *Author's collection.*

THE BUNIS *Sample* SHOP

1631 HERTEL AVE.

Open 9:30 A. M.
Until 9:30 P. M.

Please See Other "Sample Shop" News, on Page 15

Plenty of "OOMPH"

in "Sample Shop's" clever

JUNIOR FROCKS

for expensive tastes
on limited allowances

Just Arrived, and at "Sample Shop"

Exclusively **8.95** *Instead of 10.95*

Ten Styles

(Three Sketched)

Spun Rayon and Cotton

Sizes 9 to 17

Sketched Above: tri-tone stripe effect, in red, white and blue ... blue, brown and yellow ... or brown, white and lime green.

Centre Sketch: white with black and white gingham check ... or white with plain red or blue.

Sketched Left: black, aqua, powder blue or pink ... with embroidered batiste plastron.

The same day Anne started the store, her husband, Lou, started a heating business, and he worked part time helping her in the store. But business at the store was so good that he eventually closed his business and was hired by Anne to work full time for her. That first year, they did about $131,000 ($1.67 million) in sales.[136]

The Sample Shop always tried to be unique and cutting-edge, from the merchandise it carried to its marketing. "Back in the days when airplane advertising was a novelty, Sample Shop leaflets were scattered over the city by plane. When the shop still consisted of remodeled houses, it staged live fashion shows in the windows. Chairs were set on the lawn for spectators."[137]

Starting in 1929, Mrs. Bunis filed multiple business certificates covering a variety of names: Original $12.75 Sample Dress Shop, Sample Coat Shop and other variations on the name.

By this time, they had acquired the building next door at 1631 Hertel Avenue, and in 1946 their company was incorporated. The original directors of the company were Harry Serotte, Joshua Sands Jr. and Mollie J. Buscaglia.

By 1937, the company had a new façade built, joining the houses to appear to be one seamless storefront. It added more merchandise as the store grew, and it continued to burst at the seams.

The company's growth necessitated the use of the entire house, and then additions were made to the first and second floors, extending into the rear. Then yet another house next door was purchased and joined together with the original. About sixty employees were employed in 1939, which increased to over two hundred by 1946.

It was in early 1946 that the company embarked on its first major expansion, which included razing the original home and storefront, plus the razing of four other houses it had purchased.[138]

The $250,000 ($2.79 million) investment made the store 165 feet wide and 45 feet deep, with three floors of selling space. With the expansion, it added many new departments, including an infants' and children's department, a nursery, a playroom, shoes, jewelry, men's clothing and a beauty salon.[139] Several of Louis' brothers joined the company, as did Anne and Louis' son Maer.[140]

In 1933, Anne Bunis left the business to raise her children,[141] but she returned in 1950 to work in the bridal and formal departments. From the 1940s through the 1950s, the company opened a chain called Size 9 Shops with several locations, including downtown.[142]

By 1952, it had opened branches in Lancaster and Lockport, further spreading its market penetration. It celebrated its silver jubilee that year, stressing that it was still a family-owned business, with no outside interests.

In 1953, it took over the former W.T. Grant store at 2182 Seneca Street in South Buffalo. It continued to grow and in 1957 added a branch at Thruway Plaza. Always wanting a downtown location, it leased the then closing Flint & Kent store in a deal that included the entire building, employees and merchandise.

The Flint & Kent deal was a bad one, and in early 1959, the company was experiencing problems paying creditors, so it closed the downtown store and refocused its efforts.[143] Luckily for the chain, it had created a separate company, and this did not affect its overall business.

In 1961, it opened its seventh store, in Amherst. That year it also formed the Sample Casual Shops Inc., which was dissolved in 1967.

In November 1965, their son David joined the business after spending five years with Bloomingdale's in its management training program in New York City.[144] The chain again prospered, and in 1977, it merged all of its stores into the Sample Inc., with the Bunises' oldest son, Maer, as president.

By the time of its sixtieth anniversary in 1988, the company had grown to an eleven-store chain and opened its last store in the Walden Galleria Mall, adding to the $19 million ($35 million) chain.[145] In the 1980s, the company opened the Price Break, a small chain it used to sell clearance merchandise.[146]

Everything appeared to be going well for the Sample, but the savings and loan crisis that started in the late 1980s became a thorn in its, and most small retailers', sides. With credit being squeezed, Sample's bank, Liberty, stopped issuing, and it became impossible for the chain to purchase the high-quality goods in the quantities its customers desired. It was forced to buy cheaper and in less quantities, and its customers noticed the difference.

The Bunises closed their Seneca Mall store in October 1989 after opening in the Walden Galleria Mall. "We stuck it out as long as we could, but relief was not forthcoming in the form of other stores" opening in the mall, said Vice-Chairman David Bunis to the *Buffalo News*.[147]

The following month, Louis Bunis died, and ten days later, the company closed its Thruway Mall location, which was just one mile away from the Galleria and also suffered from its opening.[148] It was lured to the Galleria Mall, in a deal that included larges sums of money and a very favorable rent rate, because it needed Sample and its advertising to help promote the new mall. Maer Bunis took over as chairman at this time.

The company was down to nine stores, and in April 1990, it closed its Eastern Hills Mall location. The mall was not doing well, and Eastern Hills management wanted the space, so it let the company out of its lease.[149] The company also remodeled its flagship Hertel Avenue store. In addition, it reverted back to its original name, the Sample Shop, from just the Sample.[150]

While all these things were happening, a secret merger was taking place behind the scenes. L.L. Berger and the Sample Shop were both locally owned and experiencing the financial crisis and decided to merge to save money. Unfortunately, an agreement could not be reached between all the parties involved, and it was ended before it began.[151]

When Maer Bunis, chairman of the company, died in early 1990, David Bunis was thrust into the chairmanship role. In late August, vendors picketed the Hertel store in response to slow payments. Employment at that store dropped from 190 to 75, and the number of buyers dropped from eleven to three. The Lockport store was closed in early September, but it still wasn't enough.

David Bunis, having lost his father and brother within just three months, was given the additional task of trying to save the business. On September 12, 1990 the firm filed Chapter 11 and immediately closed the Galleria, McKinley and Northtown Plaza stores.

Down to just three stores, it struggled to adjust. "Sample was known for quality, for being the first to come out with new styles and trends. Let's hope they can bring it back," stated a department manager from the Hertel store.[152]

The final blow came just one month later as it announced that it was shutting the doors for good, with many of its creditors being clothing suppliers.[153] The last store left in the former eleven-store chain, the flagship Hertel store, closed its doors on January 31, 1991.[154] It was a sad ending for the grand clothing chain, which had expanded into the suburbs and become a profitable business only to fall victim to the savings and loan scandal.

In late December 1992, the building was sold, and the new owners built senior citizens apartments on the site.[155] Anne Bunis died in a Sarasota, Florida nursing home in 1999 at the age of ninety-eight,[156] having outlived her wonderful creation. A plaque at 1631 Hertel Avenue is all that's left of one of Buffalo's retail pioneers.

Year founded: 1928
Year closed: 1991

Other Local Stores

Krasner's was a women's clothing store started by Marvin Krasner. He opened his first store in the Southgate Plaza in West Seneca, New York, in 1956. Marvin, known as Mr. K., at one point operated stores in the Boulevard Mall, McKinley Mall and Seneca Mall, as well as Southgate Plaza. The company was one of the original tenants of the Boulevard Mall. That location closed in December 1999, leaving just the Southgate site. Krasner had invested in other properties, including the Amherst Hills Tennis Club, which he opened in 1979 with his wife. The last and original Southgate store closed in 2003, and the Krasners died weeks apart in April 2007.

The Fisher Jewelry Store opened in about 1864 at 251 Main Street in the Dennis Building. In 1914, Nate W. Weisberg purchased the store and renamed it Nate Weisberg Inc. He eventually moved to 365 Main Street and opened a branch in 1939 at 977 Broadway, the former Jahraus-Braun store. He also had four other branches. In 1940, he moved to 380 Main Street, which was later torn down to build Main Place Mall, where the company was one of the first tenants. Known as the "Watch King,"[157] he added a partner in 1954 and began mainly selling diamonds. In about 2001, it moved to Court Street. Longtime employee Edward G. Wicks purchased the business in 1979, and in January 2011, 97 years after Nate Weisberg took over and 147 years after its beginning, the doors were closed forever.

Anthony M. Peller and Paul Mure opened Peller & Mure in 1948 at 15 Court Street. The upscale men's clothing store saw many changes downtown over the years. In 1978, the company was sold to Twin Fair Inc. It moved in about 1981 to 340 Delaware Avenue, added a women's line and, almost five years later, moved to 300 Pearl Street and lastly to 19 Court Street before finally closing in 2000.

Isaac S. Given and his cousin Louis L. Berger opened a women's apparel store in Toledo, Ohio, in 1902.[158] They moved to Buffalo in 1905, and Given opened a store at 452–454 Main Street. Given's Inc. became quite popular, and the store expanded in a short time. He decided to retire in November 1928 with the store doing sales of $1.2 million ($15.3 million) per year, and he leased the operation to Miller's Inc., a national chain of stores with aspirations of three hundred stores. But financial troubles with Miller's forced Given out of retirement in 1931 to reopen the store. He continued to operate the store until poor health forced his final retirement in 1940.[159] Bond Stores took over the location that same year.

Lou Berger and his cousin Isaac Given both started women's clothing stores in downtown Buffalo after moving from Toledo. Given's was very popular until his retirement in 1928. This is one of the going-out-of-business sale newspaper ads. *Author's collection.*

In 1880, Peter Young came to the United States and settled in Buffalo, joining thousands of other Germans on the city's primarily German East Side. "Perceiving that it was as difficult to survive here as an inexperienced musician as it was in the old homeland, he opened a small men's clothing store in a house at 586 Genesee Street on June 10, 1882,"[160] selling hats and caps. By 1903, he was at 482 Genesee Street, listed as "clothing and notions,"[161] and by 1910, he had moved to a "large double building at 582 and 584 Genesee Street…considered among the largest and most renown on this main thoroughfare in the German section of the city."[162] Young manufactured his own goods, "ranging in quality from the dress suit to the working overalls, and had ten employees by 1889."[163] Before 1930, Young died, and Dorothy Matlock assumed presidency of the company. The business survived many years, several wars, the Great Depression and a changing East Side neighborhood until 1974, when it closed its doors for good. Peter Young had traveled throughout Latin America extensively, and a collection of his photographic slides is archived at University of California–Davis.[164]

Abraham Slotkin, a Russian emigrant, first appears in a Buffalo directory in 1892 as a tailor, located at 68 Mortimer Street. By 1903, he is listed selling "cloaks, millinery and furs."[165] By 1923, there were three Slotkins involved

OPEN EVERY NIGHT EXCEPT WEDNESDAY

FINAL CLEARANCE

SALE

SELECT YOUR WINTER
COAT NOW AND SAVE
ALMOST HALF . . .

UNTRIMMED COATS
FORMERLY
28.00 To 35.00 · · $18⁰⁰

FUR TRIMMED COATS
FORMERLY
68.00 To 88.00 $48⁰⁰

FUR TRIMMED COATS
FORMERLY
98.00 To 128.00 $78⁰⁰

*Plus Tax

In Most Cases These Coats Are Now
Priced Below Wholesale Cost . . . .
ACT NOW AND SAVE !!

Individually Yours

SLOTKINS

621 WILLIAM ST.

BUDGET PLAN AVAILABLE

Slotkin's was a women's clothing store started on William Street by Abraham Slotkin, who died in 1937. The business was sold to Isidor Victor Ament and later moved to East Mohawk Street. This was an early newspaper ad from when it was still located on William Street. *Author's collection.*

in the clothing trade, and Abraham had relocated to 521 William Street and to 621 William Street in 1935. The company focused on being an upscale women's dress shop. Abraham Slotkin died in 1937, and the business was sold to Isidor Victor Ament and renamed Slotkin's Inc. By 1960, the company had moved to 15 East Mohawk Street and opened a location at 3070 Bailey Avenue in Amherst. In February 1977, the company announced that it was closing both locations due to high crime—both locations had several break-ins in a seven-month period. It also said that the bus stop clogged its storefront on East Mohawk Street, discouraging patrons from entering.

"Way back in 1916 when mother was a little girl, Morrison's opened for business at 420 Main Street."[166] Started by Joseph R. Morrison, the women's clothing store featured "cloaks, suits, etc."[167] In 1920, it moved to larger quarters at 444 Main Street, and its continued success over the years allowed it to purchase the adjoining property and expand again in 1950. It added to its success by opening the Downstairs Economy Fashion Shop in 1950[168] and opened branches at 981 Broadway in Buffalo and 27 Main Street in Tonawanda. In 1962, it announced the closing of its downtown store due to "the redevelopment plan"[169] on Main Street. Two new suburban stores were announced, as was a location in the new Main Place Mall. By 1980, it had three stores, but the chain was closed before 1983.

The first Liberty Shoe Stores Inc. site was opened in 1919 at 923 Broadway by David Abrams. By 1941, there were eleven branches across

Liberty Shoes was a popular chain that grew to eleven stores in Buffalo. Known as the place to get your Chuck Taylor "Cons," this is one of its stores located in downtown Buffalo. *Courtesy of David Torke.*

the city, including one at 583 Main Street and later one at 563 Main Street. By 1961, Abrams estimated that he had sold 25 million pairs of shoes.[170] The chain was still open in 1986, but it was down to four stores as competition from national shoe chains put more pressure on it. In 1988, it closed the Grant Street store, which had been open since about 1928. The last store was closed before 1993.

In 1915, Samuel Ehrenreich was a tailor in Buffalo, located at 15 Niagara Street, and by 1918, he had opened Riverside Men's Shop at 783 Tonawanda Street, in the Riverside section of Buffalo. The company was incorporated in 1935 as Riverside Men's Quality Shop Inc., with his sons, Raymond and David, taking over. A fire nearly destroyed the company in 1940,[171] but it rebuilt, and success followed. In 1997, it opened a location in the populous Williamsville, New York, and after declining sales at the flagship Riverside location, it closed that store in 2005. The Williamsville store was still open in 2013.

One peer of Ehrenreich was Edward C. Brennan, who opened Brennan's Men's Wear, a men's furnishings store, at 2079 Niagara Street in 1915. In late 2001, current owner Bob Goulding Jr., grandson of Brennan, closed the

Although Sattler's is usually the store associated with the Broadway-Fillmore neighborhood, Posmantur's was also quite popular. Started by Russian immigrant Morris Posmantur in 1894, this was its store on Broadway next to Sattler's. *Courtesy of Christopher Byrd.*

Buffalo store and moved to 5522 Main Street in Williamsville. It announced on November 24, 2006, that it was closing its doors for good. "I'd love to continue. I want to keep going. It's not from lack of effort on my part," he said. "But Buffalo has a diminishing population. Most of my customers retired, and I don't have a lot of new customers, younger guys, coming in."[172]

Morris Posmantur arrived from Russia in 1894, a thirty-four-year-old man. A few short years later, he opened Posmantur's, a men's and boys' clothing store, at 992 Broadway. Success followed him, and he opened a store at 349 Main Street in Buffalo. In 1936, he died, and control of the business fell to his sons, Henry and Charles. They continued the operation, opening a location at 3116 Bailey Avenue, and moved the Main Street store to 523 Main Street when the land at 349 Main Street was acquired to build M&T Plaza. They were pioneers in advertising, used sports in their promotions and provided credit for purchases through their own Buffalo Budget Company.[173] Henry continued the business after his brother died and closed it upon his retirement in 1960.

Gamler's jewelry store was located next to L.L. Berger at 522 Main Street in downtown Buffalo. Its lighted sign was said to be the largest jewelry store sign in the country and could be seen for three miles. This is a great picture of both Berger's and Gamler's from the 1980s. *Courtesy of Barbara Campagna.*

Russian-born furrier Meyer Ullman is first listed in the 1898 city directory with Mary Brown as Brown & Ullman at 621 Main Street. A few short years later, he opened M. Ullman Inc. at 14 West Mohawk Street, selling wholesale furs. He moved to 246 Pearl Street and opened a retail store in 1914 on the first floor of his location at 700 Main Street. Ullman died in the late 1930s, but the operation continued on with other family members. By 1968, there is no longer any listing for Ullman.

The Gamler's Jewelers name evokes a time when you could spend your day shopping on Main Street in downtown Buffalo and leave with bags and bags of goods. Harry Gamler came to Buffalo from New York City to manage the Moses Cohen Jewelry store at 203 Main Street in 1915. When World War I began, he enlisted and served his country, returning to Buffalo afterward. Taking his separation pay, he invested in souvenir war magazines and made enough to open his first jewelry store at 11 Swan Street in 1919. He moved to 259 Main Street (also home to Kleinhans and Hengerer's) and later to 522 Main Street, across the street from Victor's.

Gamler added a giant electric street sign that had eleven thousand bulbs and "was said to be the largest sign on a jewelry store in the country and could be seen three miles away."[174] In 1968, he spent $150,000 to "modernize" the store.[175] His son, Herbert, eventually took over the business, although Harry was active until he was ninety-five years old.[176] In 1994, Herbert announced plans to move to Williamsville,[177] which seem to have fallen through, and the downtown store was closed in 1999. Gamler laid part of the blame for his business closing on downtown: "We would have been far better off if they hadn't spent the $500 million on the transit line. Why would people want to come downtown when there's free parking in the suburban malls and they feel more secure?"[178]

David's People's Store or Specialty Shop was first opened in 1925, with Peter Glick as the store manager of this women's clothing store. It was located at 555 Main Street, and by 1940, it had moved to 495 Main Street. In 1963, there were five locations, and David N. Trerotola was the vice-president and general manager. By 1980, only the Niagara Falls Boulevard location was left, and that store was closed before 1982.

August Heinrich Hoyler started in the jewelry business back in 1887. The store was located on Genesee Street. In the 1920s, a robbery resulted in the death of an employee, with one of the robbers going to the electric chair. Hoyler died in 1931, and his son, August, continued in the business, eventually opening in the Ellicott Square Building in Buffalo. His son, Charles, took over the business and opened a location in Lockport in 2012. The company is still in business today.

Many in the Seeberg family were involved in the clothing business. Harry, originally in business with his brother Edward, split to form H. Seeberg in 1936. This is a 1970s photo of the downtown store. *Courtesy of David Torke.*

Howard Jewelers Inc. was started in 1925 by Howard Duysters and William J. Kappel. "Howard Kredit Jewelers," at 5 East Genesee Street, became known for its generous credit. The company was still in business at 535 Main Street in 1993 but disappears after that.

Harry Seeberg started in the clothing business in 1927 when he and his brother, Edward, opened their own store at 340 Washington Street. In 1930, the brothers split up, and Harry started H. Seeberg Inc. at 121 Genesee Street. By 1940, Harry was president of his father's former store at 1092 Broadway, and by the time Harry died in 1962, he had opened a clothing factory and seven additional stores. The company was still in business until at least 1978, although no listing was found in 1980.

Alexander Szczukowski came to Buffalo from Poland and opened a men's clothing store at 1058 Broadway in 1890. In 1941, his son, Louis, took over the business, and then Louis' son, Louis Jr., operated the business until his death in October 2000. It is believed the family operated a location in Detroit, Michigan, at one point. After they closed, their beautiful display cases were purchased and are used today in the Buffalo Transportation Museum.

Grocery Stores and Drugstores

Buffalo is a fickle market, and there's just no [consumer] *loyalty anymore.*[179]
—Richard C. Paul, former president of Ulbrich's

Food is an essential part of our lives. We eat for nourishment as well as for pleasure, and everyone must buy groceries at one time or another. In the "glory days" of shopping, grocery stores were located in your neighborhood. You would often visit several stores to get all your needs—the butcher, the bakery, the seafood store and more.

Today's supermarkets are nothing like the stores of days past, with so many varieties and so many aisles under one roof. We often end up getting lost or spending much more money than we intended.

The drugstore was also a different place. It was often a soda fountain, a place to hang out for an ice cream and pick up your prescription. Many times, it was the one place where people of all races comingled. As the chain stores started moving into the area, the local stores started closing or selling out to them.

As supermarkets became increasingly popular, nearly every local department store opened a drug or grocery outlet at one time or another. AM&A's, Sattler's, Hengerer's, J.N.'s, Larkin, Twin Fair and today's Walmart, Target and Kmart and many others also have them.

This chapter shows the succession that many of them had over the years. Some of these stores and companies you may have heard of, and some you probably haven't. But their unique histories provide for an interesting addition to Buffalo's retailing growth.

DANAHY-FAXON, LARKIN, NU-WAY AND ACME

William Faxon came to Buffalo in 1889 and began work for a wholesale grocer. Six months after starting, his employer died, so William and his childhood friend Frederick Coffin Williams took over the business at 391 and 393 Main Street.[180]

William's son, William Alec Faxon, joined the firm, and the company became Faxon, Williams & Faxon. By 1899, there were four locations, and it had the slogan "Largest druggists. Popular prices."[181]

In 1917, Alec Faxon died, followed two years later by Frederick Williams, leaving William Faxon in charge of the company. He formed another company, Faxon United Stores Inc., and developed a mail-order business in wine and imported delicacies, known as "one of the finest grocery, cigar, wine and imported foodstuff store in western New York."[182] It would grow to an impressive forty-eight stores.

Edward T. Danahy was born into the meat business as a member of Buffalo's Danahy family. By 1910, he was operating E.T. Danahy Company meat markets, with offices at 49 West Chippewa Street, and by 1920, it was a meat and grocery store.

Thrift Grocery Stores Inc. started in about 1918 with a location at 460 Main Street in the basement of the former H.A. Meldrum store. It was a self-service grocery store, with Thomas P. Cauley as the manager, and early company management included Jacob Gerhard Lang. Shortly after the end of World War I, Faxon sold his company to Thrift, and it was renamed Faxon United Stores Inc., the largest grocery trade transaction in Buffalo history, creating a chain of more than eighty stores.[183]

In July 1928, Faxon, Williams & Faxon Stores, the Faxon United Stores Inc. and the Thrift Grocery Stores Inc. were merged together to form the 102-store chain known as Thrift Grocery Stores Inc. The chains had been owned by the same people but run separately.[184]

Both Faxon United and Danahy were on fast-growth tracks, and in early July 1929, the merger of the packing plant and the grocery store firms was announced. The new $1 million 130-branch company was named Danahy-Faxon Stores Inc., with Edward Danahy as president and Thomas Cauley as vice-president, until June 1931, when Cauley ascended to president.

Another business that had been very successful in Buffalo was the Larkin Company. It had been a large mail-order company that began diversifying operations as sales of its catalogue business began to wane.

This is the inside of a typical Faxon, Williams & Faxon grocery store in Buffalo. It later merged with Danahy and became Nu-Way and then Acme. *Author's collection.*

This is a great drawing for the proposed Danahy-Faxon warehouse and grocery store located on Broadway at the corner of Bailey Avenue in Buffalo. It later became Acme. *Courtesy of John and Mary Neumann.*

In 1918, it opened its first Larkin Economy Store in Buffalo to serve as an outlet for its surplus stock.[185] By 1929, it had added baked goods and meats, as well as greens in 1930. In 1920, it opened a branch in Peoria, Illinois, and by 1932 had 75 stores in Peoria and 103 stores in Western New York.

Danahy-Faxon had grown to 147 stores by 1937, when it purchased the remainder of the Larkin Food Stores Inc. chain, many stores of which were located in small agricultural towns. "More than 90 percent of our retail stores are within the city limits," stated Thomas Cauley of Danahy-Faxon at a meeting of the employees of the Larkin stores. "With the acquisition [of the Larkin stores]…a more even balance will be maintained."[186] Most became Danahy-Faxon stores.

In 1938, the chain opened a new type of grocery store and named it Nu-Way Market. This new supermarket was larger than the typical Danahy-Faxon store. By 1940, there were seven locations, with a total of twenty-four local stores by 1950. The growth of the grocery chain did not go unnoticed. In 1946, American Stores Company of Philadelphia purchased Danahy-Faxon, adding to the two-thousand-plus stores it owned. Thomas Cauley was kept as president of the Danahy-Faxon division and eventually ascended to chairman of the chain.

By 1960, there were twenty local Nu-Way stores, eighty in total, and the Danahy-Faxon brand was no more. The following year, American Stores Company re-branded the chain, naming the stores Acme after the company's brand in Philadelphia. Acme had a nice run in Buffalo, operating branches throughout the city and suburbs until July 1979, when the company announced that it was pulling out of the Buffalo and Syracuse markets, closing forty-five stores, fifteen locally. Local competitor Bells ran a full-page ad claiming that double coupons were the reason Acme was closing. But company president Peter McGoldrick denied that, saying, "We were guilty in the '70s of neglecting our facilities. They grew old." Management didn't want to spend money on remodeling and said that the high costs from unions, especially meat cutters, were another reason it was closing the stores.[187] All the stores wouldn't be closed for long, as local chains Tops and Super Duper were both interested in the stores that would be closed.[188]

Year founded: 1889
Year closed: 1979

PETER J. SCHMITT, LOBLAWS AND BELLS

In about 1850, future mayor of Buffalo Philip Becker "became employed by Seibel & Company, his uncle being the senior partner of the company, where he was made chief clerk. After about a year, he went to work for A.P. Yaw [& Sons], a grocer on Main Street near the dock, where he remained for three years."[189]

In 1854, Becker opened a grocery business at 390 Main Street between Mohawk and Genesee Streets. He remained there for four years, at which time he moved to larger quarters at 384 Main Street. Business increased, and in 1861, Becker purchased the site at 468 and 470 Main Street, where the business was moved. With the addition of partners, the firm was now called Philip Becker & Company.

Becker remained president of the firm until about 1888, at which time he was in the midst of his third term as mayor of Buffalo. Arthur Groben was president of the firm until about 1920, and John G. Wickson had been added to the firm as vice-president in about 1915, rising to the presidency in 1925. In the meantime, the company had moved to 266 Pearl Street and then to Perry Street, corner of Michigan Avenue.

In 1883, Civil War veteran Jerome I. Prentiss was involved in Prentiss & Loveland, commercial merchants, with a location at 98 West Market Street. By 1897, the company was named J.I. Prentiss & Company, wholesale grocers, located at Michigan Avenue and Perry Street. When Prentiss was ready to retire in 1920, he merged the company with Becker's, forming Becker Prentiss Inc.[190] In 1944, it became a division of Francis H. Leggett & Company,[191] and in 1958, Leggett was bought by Peter J. Schmitt Company and promptly closed.[192]

The Schmitt story starts in the 1890s when Joseph Schmitt sold his small grocery store to his son, Peter, so he could concentrate on other interests.[193] By 1921, Peter had expanded the business to eight stores, and shortly afterward, he decided to start a wholesale operation in the back of one store. In 1925, he shut down his stores to work full time at the wholesale side; in 1927, his Fidelity Grocers Supply Company was located at 495 Goodyear Avenue. The company continued to grow, eventually supplying local IGA, Bells and Twin Fair grocery stores.[194]

In 1925, Toronto, Canada grocer Theodore P. Loblaw expanded his growing food chain into Buffalo, opening three Loblaw Groceterias in the city. By 1940, there were thirty-five branches in Buffalo, which became the United States headquarters for Loblaws Inc. By 1946, ninety-three stores were being serviced from the Buffalo warehouse. In 1947, the company was purchased by George Weston Ltd. of Canada,[195] and in 1953, it announced plans to open eight new local stores. Weston built Loblaws into Canada's largest grocery chain, buying up other chains and products.

Bells was a Buffalo-based grocery chain started in 1954 when ten independent stores merged. They were supplied by the Peter J. Schmitt Company, which also owned Loblaws at the time. This is one of the later Bells logos. *Author's collection.*

In 1962, Star Discount Foods appeared in Western New York and often advertised alongside Loblaws. A year later, Star had eleven stores from Niagara Falls to Lancaster, with several in the city of Buffalo. By 1963, there were ads touting Loblaw-Star, but Star Discount Foods continued to advertise until at least the late 1960s. It was during this time that ownership was confirmed as being Loblaws.

Along the way, Loblaws purchased a Buffalo-based company in a hush-hush deal. The Canadian conglomerate did not want anyone to know that it had privately bought Peter J. Schmitt from the controlling family in 1966[196] and now owned two competing supermarkets in the Buffalo area.[197]

Bells was a grocery chain well remembered by many Buffalonians. The chain was founded in 1954 by the merging of ten independent stores with a goal to "keep the personal tone of operation while achieving a uniformity of prices."[198] The ten stores were all over Erie County, from the city of Buffalo to the town of East Aurora. It was officially incorporated in October 1959.

Bells was organized and supplied by the Peter J. Schmitt Company, which prepared and controlled all aspects of its advertising and pricing. Additionally, Schmitt opened several Bells stores that were company-run as the chain expanded in the 1960s and '70s. By 1965, Bells had thirty stores in Western New York.[199]

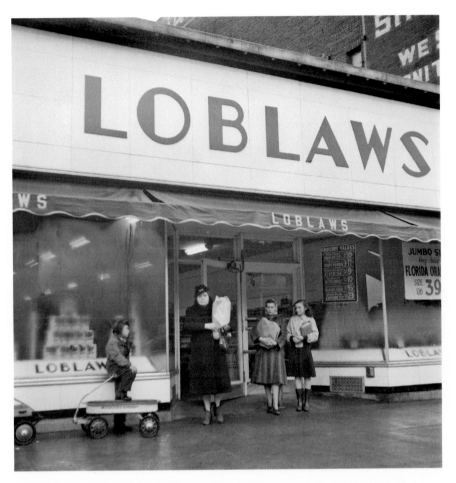

This picture is of a young boy waiting outside a Loblaws store in Buffalo to drum up business for his grocery delivery. Taken in 1944, he used the money to help pay for his school supplies. *Courtesy of Library of Congress, Prints & Photographs Division, FSA/OWI Collection, reproduction number LC-USF34-9058-C.*

In 1973, Loblaws announced the closing of four local stores, and by 1975, there were just seven Loblaws stores in Buffalo. In 1974, George Weston Ltd. finally admitted that it owned both Bells and Loblaws after a real estate transaction between the two companies came to light.[200]

In September 1975, Weston decided to shift Loblaws distribution to Peter J. Schmitt, and a few months later, in January 1976, it decided to close all the Buffalo-area Loblaws stores. The next month, Bells announced plans to reopen twenty-one of the closing Loblaws stores as Bells. The seesaw ride was far from over, though.

Bells supermarkets ran a promotion with the Buffalo Bills football team for the Whammy, made to intimidate opposing teams and neutralize other "inferior" team mascots. *Author's collection.*

With other local grocery chains such as Tops Markets, Super Duper and Wegmans of Rochester moving in, Bells had its work cut out for it. When the 1980s arrived, Bells began closing unprofitable stores. In 1988, "a group of senior managers [headed by Charles Barcelona]...purchased Peter J. Schmitt from George Weston Ltd."[201] It restructured the company, eliminated one division and laid off employees. The plan didn't work, and in May 1992, it filed for bankruptcy protection under Chapter 11.[202] It eventually exited bankruptcy. "The extended deep recession...has made it increasingly difficult...to compete in its markets,"[203] along with poor business decisions that expanded the company and depleted its profits. These included investing outside its market area where it didn't know the business climate well enough.

The recession that started with 1987's "Black Friday" continued to plague Western New York well into the 1990s. Bells decided to push its generic product offerings in early 1992 in the hopes that it would increase sales and help the no. 3 supermarket chain in Western New York.

Instead, December 1992 was a sad month for Buffalo-area residents as Schmitt announced that it was closing all sixty-one Bells supermarkets in an attempt to avoid bankruptcy. Scrivner Inc., which operated Super Duper and Jubilee Foods, purchased thirty-three stores and the Bells name,[204] and Penn Traffic Company, which operated Quality Markets, purchased twenty-eight stores.[205]

Peter J. Schmitt Inc., the former billion-dollar company, ended up closing all its warehouse and distribution facilities and reorganizing as an asset and property management company.[206] As of 1996, it was still being liquidated.

Year founded: 1854
Year closed: 1992

RED & WHITE, SUPER DUPER, JUBILEE AND QUALITY

Smith M. Flickinger started what would be Buffalo's first billion-dollar company in 1903 when he opened his wholesale grocery business with $16,000 he had saved. The growing company built a warehouse at Perry and Illinois Streets in 1911 and bought or opened branches throughout upstate New York, Pennsylvania and Ohio.[207]

The company supplied groceries to independent grocery stores, and during World War I, the pressure on the small stores increased as food was rationed. By this time, the company was operating its own chain of Flickinger's retail stores, as well as the wholesale operation supplying others.

In 1921, Smith Flickinger came up with a plan to compete with other chains, such as the Great Atlantic & Pacific Tea Company, and create new business owners. Flickinger basically started an early franchise operation that included site selection, training and discounted fixture purchases. Using the knowledge that he had developed, the company used professional window display men and helped to properly stock the store for its initial opening to avoid "the failure of thousands of corner grocers."[208] The result was the Red & White Food Stores chain.

The Red & White chain spawned its own food brands, such as the Red & White, Blue & White, Our Value and Brimfull brands. By 1935, there were 14 Red & White stores in the Buffalo area and 212 by 1947; the company had expanded exponentially, with 6,500 stores in thirty-three states and across Canada.[209] The corporation was eventually headquartered in Chicago, with offices in Buffalo.

This is the logo for Super Duper, a popular Buffalo grocery chain. People often remember its spokeswoman "Joey" and its elephant mascot. *Author's collection.*

In 1957, Flickinger unveiled a new grocery store concept known as Super Duper. This store was the next-generation Red & White grocery store, and newspaper ads started incorporating both names until late 1957, when Super Duper was the only name, and R&W Super Markets Inc. officially became Super Duper Inc., although Red & White still had stores open into the 1970s. In 1975, "Flickinger took over several A&P stores in western New York…who then made them into Super Duper stores."[210]

By 1984, the S.M. Flickinger Company was a $1 billion ($2.1 billion) company, operating out of a huge warehouse built in 1961 in Cheektowaga. At this time, Scrivner Inc. came calling, and Flickinger was sold. Burt P. Flickinger Jr., son of the founder, stayed on as president

This is a great photo of Super Duper, with a truck with the Red & White logo on it. You can see the dancing elephant on the building sign. *Courtesy of Ken Goudy.*

of the Flickinger division until his retirement in 1991, at which time the division was given the Scrivner name.[211] Shortly afterward, Scrivner pushed the independent Super Duper stores to adopt its Jubilee store concept and officially dissolved the Super Duper corporation in August 1991. In September 1992, fifteen stores switched over, and in January 1993, seven more made the switch. Between 1991 and 1992, many Super Duper stores also closed, leaving some neighborhoods without any grocery stores.

Quality Markets, which was owned by Penn Traffic Company of Pennsylvania, saw an opportunity to enter the Buffalo market when Bells and Super Duper closed, and it purchased twenty-eight Super Duper stores in 1992.

In July 1994, Fleming Company merged with Scrivner Inc., creating the country's largest grocery wholesaler.[212] The Buffalo market was now consolidated to four major players: Tops Markets, Wegmans, Quality

Markets and Jubilee Foods. Quality and Jubilee began closing unprofitable stores throughout the 1990s, and in 1995, Quality bought seven Jubilee stores and closed one.

The next several years were rocky in the grocery business as Jubilee Foods and Quality Markets continued to pare down their operations to the most profitable stores. Quality purchased more Jubilee stores and closed additional Quality sites. In 1999, Fleming Company closed six Jubilee stores, and the following year, it announced that it was completely pulling out of the Buffalo area in order to concentrate on other aspects of its conglomerate. The local Jubilee stores were split, some sold and some closed. In 2006, there was one local Jubilee store. That was sold to Tops in 2010 and remodeled into a Tops store.

Penn Traffic went through Chapter 11 bankruptcy protection in 1999 and closed more than forty-eight stores. In May 2003, it again entered Chapter 11, eventually closing more than one hundred more stores. In 2006, there was one local Quality Markets store. In January 2010, Tops purchased the bankrupt Penn Traffic, including seventy-nine Quality stores.

To no one's surprise, Fleming also filed Chapter 11 for bankruptcy protection in April 2003, after losing a lucrative contract with Kmart, and sold its wholesale unit to four different companies.

Year founded: 1903
Year closed: 2010

TOPS MARKETS

Writing about Tops Friendly Markets (known by most as Tops Markets, or Tops) was an interesting task. What section should it be put in, since it was started in Niagara Falls and matured in Buffalo and since the headquarters moved to Europe and then returned to Buffalo? It's the largest supermarket chain in Western New York in terms of sales volume and number of stores, but its state of popularity is always up for discussion. By default, it is the store where most people shop.

It all started in about 1925 when Ferranti Castellanti opened a grocery store in Niagara Falls, at Garden and Highland Streets. When he died in 1933, his son, Armand, quit school to help run it.[213] The business was sold in 1941, and Armand and his brother opened Big Bear Markets in Niagara Falls.

Tops Friendly Markets began in Niagara Falls when some like-minded men decided to open a new type of grocery store. Today, it is the largest grocery chain in Western New York. This is a late 1960s logo. *Author's collection.*

As the business grew, it expanded and moved several times, eventually working with Thomas A. Buscaglia to form the T.A. Buscaglia Equipment Company.[214] In 1953, Thomas and his brother, John, as well as two others, formed Niagara Frontier Services, which sold refrigeration products to grocery stores and would eventually become the parent of Tops.[215] They convinced the owners of four Bells Markets (including the Coopers, who were also Bells' founders) to join them in a new supermarket concept. They converted a store on Hyde Park Boulevard in Niagara Falls and opened it in 1956.[216]

The group opened several more Bells stores, finally opening the largest in 1960 at Portage and Cedar Roads in Niagara Falls. The group decided to split with the Peter J. Schmitt Company, which supplied Bells, and went with S.M. Flickinger Company, supplier for Red & White and Super Duper. In 1958, Buscaglia purchased thirty acres of land in Buffalo on Dingens Street, which would become the company's headquarters. At that time, Savino Nanula and the others decided that the time was right to incorporate, and in February 1960, Tops Inc. was formed.[217]

The company had three Tops Markets in operation in Niagara Falls when it decided to move into the Buffalo market. It worked with its former Bells partners and converted several Bells stores into Tops. In 1962, the company formed Niagara Frontier Services Inc. (better known as NFS) as the parent company.

It began franchising Tops stores and B-Kwik, a smaller concept store, and in 1972, it merged about fifteen stores into the parent company so they were company-owned. By 1975, it had twenty-three company-owned and twenty-four franchised stores. In 1969, it expanded to Erie, Pennsylvania, and also opened its first Wilson Farms Neighborhood Food Store (a convenience store) in Tonawanda,[218] and in 1975, it expanded Tops to Rochester, New York.

In 1969, Tops launched Wilson Farms, a convenience store chain that would become successful and the biggest convenience chain in Western New York. In 1968, Tops began trading on the American Stock Exchange.[219] This would eventually attract the attention of outside investors, and in 1978, Buffalo-based Sportservice Inc. (headed by the Jacobs family) was poised to purchase the company but decided against the purchase.

That changed in 1987 as an investment group headed by Freeman Spogli & Company purchased the company for $200 million.[220] Just a few years later, in 1991, Royal Ahold, a major Netherlands food retailer, purchased the company. The company moved from its longtime headquarters in Buffalo to a new building in the suburb of Williamsville, New York, in 1994 and built a super distribution center in Lancaster, New York, two years later.[221]

Tops continued expanding, merging with other chains that Ahold owned and purchasing additional chains. But all this growth was not without changes to the former locally owned company. The company sold all three distribution facilities it owned in 2002, including the Lancaster site, shifted many office jobs to other divisions out of state[222] and, in 2003, announced that a probe at Ahold had uncovered $800 million in understatements, $29 million attributed to Tops.[223] This forced the company to sell off assets, including Wilson Farms in 2005[224] and Tops stores in areas in which they weren't already market leaders. In November 2006, Ahold announced that the Tops chain was for sale.

In 2005, Wilson Farms and Sugar Creek stores were purchased from Tops by a local investment group headed by the Nanula family, and in April 2011, they in turn sold Wilson Farms to Dallas-based 7-Eleven, which re-branded the stores as such.

In October 2007, Morgan Stanley Private Equity announced that it was purchasing Tops from Ahold for $310 million and returned management to Buffalo.[225] It planned on keeping the company in its portfolio for the long term. In January 2010, it purchased the bankrupt Penn Traffic seventy-nine-store chain that included Quality Markets. It closed twenty-four of the stores and remodeled many as Tops stores.[226]

Today, Tops is once again locally run and is still the dominant grocery chain in the Buffalo area.

Year founded: 1925
Still open in 2013

Other Local Stores

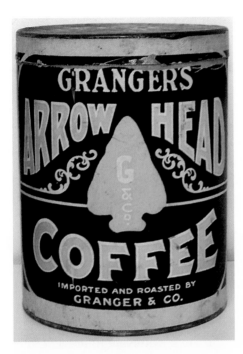

The Arrowhead Food Stores chain had grown to eight hundred stores by 1926. Some of its popular coffee brands included Granger's, Royal Blend and Eureka. *Author's collection.*

Granger & Company wholesale grocers was started in Painesville, Ohio, in about 1853 by William and Edmond W. Granger. In 1872, they moved to Buffalo, where they continued in the wholesale business. In about 1885, the partnership dissolved, with Edmond retaining the business name. By 1895, Granger and his son-in-law, Charles Townsend Wilson, were manufacturing baking powder and mustard and sold whiskey, spices and roasted coffee. In 1925, the Granger Company Inc. was formed through the merger of Cumpson-Doelman & Company, Peterson-Weter Company and Granger & Company, with warehouse and offices at 135 Scott Street. The company would be worth $13 million today and, much like Red & White Food Stores, formed Arrowhead Stores Corporation, a volunteer organization that in 1926 had one thousand individually owned and operated stores in Western New York.[227] "The tremendous quantity buying power of Arrowhead Stores assures everyone the very best food products at moderate prices."[228]

The company said that it "pioneered the cooperative buying idea for the independent grocer."[229] "[They] were leaders in the coffee roasting industry," including Royal Blend coffee,[230] and Granger's brand items. There were dozens of stores in Niagara Falls, as well as across the state. Granger's items can be found for sale on Internet sites. Arrowhead was still advertising in 1951, but the number of stores seems to have declined considerably by this time. It is unknown when the chain ceased operations.

Other local grocery stores were Keller Brothers' Jumbo Markets and Harvest stores. Each had multiple locations.

DRUGSTORES

Cyrenius C. Bristol was a descendant of one of the earliest families of Buffalo, New York.[231] In the drug field, he was best known for Bristol's Sarsaparilla, and he is credited with having originated the patent medicine almanac, along with other advertising innovations.[232] From 1854 to 1861, Bristol was owner and publisher of the *Buffalo Republic* newspaper. In 1848, Oliver H.P. Champlin, who had been working in Bristol's store as a bookkeeper, set out on his own as a druggist, opening Champlin & Company.

By 1875, Thomas Stoddart was a partner in the business with Champlin at 75 East Seneca Street. A few years later, Stoddart's brother, Charles, also a druggist, joined him, and they opened up Stoddart Brothers Inc. at 84 East Seneca Street. The business proved to be quite successful, and by 1930, they had a few branch stores.

Stoddart Brothers is said to be the first store in Buffalo to install a soda fountain, and it is one of a handful in the country that claim to have made the first ice cream sundae. Its claim was beat by more than fifteen years, but it may have been the first in Buffalo to make the cold concoction. By 1942, there was only one location, at 86 Seneca Street. But time had run out on Stoddart Brothers, and it was closed by 1946.

Another firm that mirrored the longevity of Stoddart Brothers was Heegaard-Miller. Aage C. Heegaard located his shop at 778 Genesee Street in 1889. By 1908, he had three locations, and in 1920, he paired up with Sloan. By 1930, they were with Edgar F. Miller, and it became Heegaard-Miller Drug Company, with another location at 603 Genesee Street. In 1966, 603 Genesee Street was closed, and by 1973, Legrand L. Hall was the owner. Hall also owned Hall's Pharmacy in North Tonawanda. In 1982, there is no listing for Heegaard-Miller, but Hall was located at 852 East Delavan Avenue.

In 1899, druggist G.B. Rogers was located at 402 Michigan Avenue. In December 1918, he was bought out by Harry V. Rosokoff, Dr. Lester I. Levyn, Joseph Schweitzer and Dr. George E. Slotkin, who in turn opened what was one of the first all-night pharmacies in the country, Rogers-Smith Drug Company Inc.

Cyrenius C. Bristol is best known for Bristol's Sarsaparilla, but he is also credited with having originated the patent medicine almanac, along with other advertising innovations. *Author's collection.*

Harvey & Carey was a popular drugstore chain in the Buffalo area. This is from a newspaper advertisement. *Author's collection.*

Dr. Slotkin invented an artificial kidney and was a professor at University at Buffalo, and Schweitzer is listed as the first president of the company, with Rosokoff the manager. The company moved north to 163 Broadway at Michigan Avenue in about 1920. Henry Schaefer was president at that time.

Schaefer continued to run the company until the business was sold, in about 1989, to Lonnie Carter, who had been manager and vice-president for several years. Mr. Carter changed the name of the pharmacy to Broadway Prescription Center and continued operating the business until he was accused of illegally dispensing more than 300,000 doses of Valium, codeine and other controlled substances in 1995. He subsequently closed the business.

Harvey & Carey Inc. was another popular chain with roots not in Buffalo. The company started in 1898 in Cattaraugus County, New York, and was incorporated in 1916. In 1923, it opened its first Buffalo location at 327 Elm Street and added additional stores until the 1950s, when it was sold to Lee's Drug Stores Inc. of Rhode Island. By 1971, it had been renamed Lee's Harvey & Carey, and in 1980, there is no listing.[233] In 1986, the corporation was inactive.

Other drugstores of note include Parsons & Judd, which had three locations in South Buffalo. It operated from about 1930 until the 1970s. Fay's was a chain that started in 1958 and eventually opened stores in the 1980s in the Buffalo area. In 1996, the chain was sold to J.C. Penney, which changed it into Eckerds.[234] It was later purchased by Rite Aid.

Sattler's operated nine drugstores, four free-standing, for about thirty years. Hens & Kelly had a pharmacy in 1905, and Tops Markets and Wegmans both operate pharmacies. Tops also operated the Vix Deep Discount drugstore chain for several years, until selling it to Drug Emporium.

There was also Ford's Cut Rate Stores Inc., operating from the late 1930s until the late 1960s, and Leader Drug Stores, a pharmacy cooperative popular from the 1950s through the 1980s. It is still in business and owned by Cardinal Health, although there may not be any Buffalo area stores open any longer.

Hardware and Home Furnishings

B uffalo has one of the oldest stock of houses in the United States. Therefore, the need to repair them is a constant battle for those who own them. This chapter covers the home in one way or another. Furniture stores and factories, appliance stores, hardware stores and factories—Buffalo once had an abundant supply of them.

At one time, there were dozens of these kinds of stores, most locally owned. As time went on, the market changed. One of the first events was the exodus to the suburbs, which moved the people farther from the stores. Then there was the arrival of the chain stores, and lastly, as for many of the stores, there were either poor market conditions or poor business decisions.

The idea of the lifetime service guarantee was apparently something unique to Buffalo. Whose lifetime was it guaranteed for? As cheaper, disposable products became more widely sold by manufacturers, it became more difficult and expensive for the retailer offering the free service to live up to that guarantee. In the end, those costs and the never-ending influx of chain stores killed almost all of the local appliance retailers.

DENTON, COTTIER & DANIELS

There is one music store in the Buffalo area with a long and varied history, starting when James D. Sheppard, born in England, came to Buffalo in 1827, lugging a piano in a boat along the Erie Canal. The piano, thought to be the first in Buffalo, was set up in the Eagle Tavern, located on the west side of Main Street south of Court Street. Sheppard later opened a music store on the location of the current downtown Buffalo library. He was a trained musician and was known as the "Father of Music in Buffalo."[236]

Later, the business was located at 266 Main Street, on the corner of Niagara Street. During the 1850s, Hugh Cottier moved to Buffalo from New York City and became Sheppard's partner. The firm of Sheppard & Cottier

This is the Denton, Cottier & Daniels building in 1902 at 269–71 Main Street in Buffalo. Today, it is the oldest Steinway piano dealer in the world. *Author's collection.*

dealt in musical instruments and music. In 1858, the firm moved to 215 Main Street, and the number changed to 269 Main Street after 1868. It stayed there for fifty years, occupying all five floors, "until construction in 1908 of the five-story musical emporium"[237] at 32–38 Court Street.

In 1863, Robert Denton joined the firm, now named Sheppard, Cottier & Company. Denton "was well known as an accomplished organist and music teacher. The business' great growth to a large extent can be attributed to Mr. Denton's popularity."[238] It actively published sheet music, some of which is in the Library of Congress. It was known as Sheppard, Cottier & Company until 1867, when James Sheppard died. At that time, the firm was renamed Cottier & Denton.[239]

William H. Daniels was the last to join the firm, in about 1872. In 1887, the firm was renamed Denton, Cottier & Daniels. Daniels would be elected Erie County treasurer in the early 1900s. The firm was a major importer of musical instruments, supplies and sheet music, as well as being music publishers.[240]

The business survived changes downtown until finally moving to the Northtown Plaza in 1976. In 1999, the business moved to Getzville, New York, closer to "Amherst and Clarence…where the most of our new customers are coming from."[241] It is still in business today and is the oldest Steinway dealer in the world.

JOHN HENRICH COMPANY

In 1867, John Henrich was a tinsmith in the growing city of Buffalo, located at 301 William Street. He handmade items such as buckets, water dippers and tea kettles, all of which he sold in his store.[242] He "made his living as a traveling tinsmith in the German neighborhood of East Buffalo. He would push his cart up and down the streets fixing pots and pans brought to him by the housewives of the neighborhood."[243] By 1886, with business prospering, he was able to purchase property located at 322 William Street to expand the business. The location had been a beer garden, which he razed to build a new store and factory.

The business grew and diversified its offerings, specializing in wood and coal heating and cookstoves. Apparently, the street numbering changed in the late 1920s, as 322 William Street became number 422.

In 1908, John died, and his son, Louis, took helm of the company. At just twenty-five years of age, he continued the growth of the company, eventually purchasing 426–428 William Street and 49 Spring Street for a warehouse. "The Great Depression nearly sank the company."[244]

In 1945, Louis started Lee Distributing Company Inc., a wholesaler of household appliances, at 845 Washington Street. "Lee Distributing became the main small appliance distributorship for all of Central and Western New York, and North Western Pennsylvania."[245] By 1947, the company's wholesale business exceeded the retail trade, with sales eclipsing $1 million ($9.76 million) per year.

In 1964, Louis died, and his son, Ralph, in turn took over the operation. He was able to keep the company in business as the face of retailing was changing in Buffalo, probably through the wholesaling side. With a changing neighborhood, "break-ins and the looting during the Blizzard of 1977 took their shots and finally convinced Ralph and [his son] John W. to close the retail store in 1982 ending 115 years of reliable neighborhood service."[246]

In 1988, Ralph died, and his son, John W. Henrich, in turn took over. In 1990, Lee Distributing was manufacturing kitchen cabinets, and before 1997, the company closed, ending another era in Buffalo retailing. Adam G. Heinrich, the great-great-grandson of John, chose to resurrect the family company name in June 2010 and opened a gun shop in suburban Western New York.[247]

Year founded: 1867
Year closed: 1982

LAURENS ENOS COMPANY

Charles F. Bricka opened the C.F. Bricka & Company furniture store in 1884, in rooms 7 and 10 over 16 East Eagle Street. Shortly afterward, he was joined by Laurens Enos, and the firm name changed to Bricka & Enos. The store grew and moved to Washington Street and eventually 621 Main Street, as the business outgrew each subsequent building. In 1918, Bricka retired and sold his interests to Enos, and the company was renamed the Laurens Enos Company Inc.

In 1923, Mr. Enos purchased the building at 621–623 Main Street. "It is not far off when Main Street, north of Chippewa, will be the heart of Buffalo's business section," Enos stated.[248]

Enos decided to retire in 1933, noting that "nearly a half century of hard work takes its toll,"[249] and he gave the business to his nephews, Edward P. Wilgus and Laurens Enos Wilgus. To expedite the process, he held a liquidation sale, with "drastic price-cuts. It is my farewell gift to Buffalo."[250]

Before his death in 1944, he had become involved in the Market Furniture Company with his nephew Laurens at 628 Washington Street.

Year founded: 1884
Year closed: 1933

SIEGRIST FURNITURE CORPORATION

Jacob J. Siegrist started working for the Barnes, Bancroft & Company department store in 1877. He advanced until he was a buyer and manager. In 1891, he became acquainted with George K. Fraley, who had a large store on Sixth Avenue in New York City. On August 6, 1891, they opened Siegrist & Fraley department store at 514–518 William Street on Buffalo's East Side. "In 1895 the firm opened a second large warehouse on Broadway (1018–1028) across the street from the Broadway Market between Peck and Mills Streets."[251]

The following year, the business was further expanded when it "took over the entire block at the corner of William and Emslie Streets and built a large, modern warehouse. The large department store and warehouse take up 3 floors of the huge building. There are 250 clerks employed there."[252]

Siegrist was a Buffalo mayoral candidate in 1909, losing by 1,239 votes.[253] In March 1920, the partners sold out to W.A. Morgan and retired. The following year, Mr. Morgan retired, and Siegrist opened J.J. Siegrist & Company Inc. It closed the Broadway store in 1921.

In 1928, seeing the sales in home furnishings outpacing the other departments, Siegrist changed the department store to a home furnishings store. In 1932, Siegrist decided to retire. His only heir, a son-in-law, had died, leaving no family member to run the business. The company was taken over by William H. Chur, who had been with the organization since 1914, and he renamed the company Siegrist Furniture Corporation. "The Siegrist store in William Street once was the Saturday-night gathering place for the whole East Side," Mr. Chur later recalled.[254]

The company remained under his control until 1946, when Chur sold it to Sidney Freedman. Earlier that same year, Jacob Siegrist had died. The store closed in about 1947, and "America's Largest Colored Owned Department Store," the J.J. Allen & Company Inc., opened in the location for a few years.

Year founded: 1891
Year closed: 1947 or 1948

THE HOME OF LIFETIME SERVICE

As televisions and radios became more popular, along with in-home washers and dryers, the need for retailers that sold those electric appliances increased. For some reason, Buffalo has always been a battle ground for appliance retailers, so it has seen its fair share of chain stores come and go.

There were numerous appliance dealers in the Buffalo area, including Kolipinski's, A to Z TV, Foster-Bodie, Bestway Stores, Maisel and Zolte, and of course, the department stores also sold appliances. Later, there were Silo's, Highland Superstores, Sun Television and Appliances, Madd Maxx, Lechmere, Rosa's, Circuit City, Orville's, Best Buy and another chain that opened in 2011 for six months. The chains come in like lions and rustle all the feathers, and nearly every one of them goes belly up.

Something unique to Buffalo was the "lifetime service guarantee," started in 1944 by Electra-Gas Appliance Corporation. Many other local dealers copied the concept. The problem was that they rarely lived up to it. Foster-Bodie closed in 1980, Burnham's in January 1989 and Electra-Gas in February 1990. Their closings left thousands of consumers with useless contracts. A to Z TV was one of the first when it closed in 1981, leaving twenty-six thousand unhappy customers.

Unfortunately for the mom and pops, or even the big Buffalo stores, the chains adversely affected the landscape during the time they were in Buffalo. All of the names we grew up with suffered from the constant pummeling from the bigger chains. We can lament their passing, but maybe we should have shopped there instead of running out to grab that discounted television from the chain store. Maybe a trip to the old East Side neighborhood to buy that refrigerator would have helped keep them in business. Just maybe.

Local outlets did exist and lasted for quite a few years until the competition from chains and the changing population drove them out of business. One of the earliest started as Wullenweber & Burnham, dealers in railroad watches and diamonds, located at 57–59 East Genesee Street. The partners were Arthur B. Burnham and Oscar Wullenweber. By 1928, it was the Bush-Burnham Company at 136 Exchange Street, and in 1935, it became Burnham's Jewelry Company, located at 1040 Broadway. By 1948, it had become Burnham's Jewelry & Furniture Company, located at 592 Walden Avenue. When Burnham's son, John, took over, it became J. Burnham's Inc. and moved to 578 Walden Avenue, later opening branches at 1209 Broadway and suburban locations. In January 1989, it shut down all the stores.[255] The Broadway location became senior citizen housing in 1998.

In 1944, Matthew Joseffer opened Electra-Gas Appliance Corporation at 421–423 Genesee Street, which became known as "the home of Lifetime Service." A few years later, he was joined by Theodore Weber, and together their lifetime service guarantee pressed other local dealers to offer similar guarantees. When you purchased a product in 1944, chances are that it was made to last, so warranty repairs may not have been as numerous as they are today with throwaway electronics. The store moved to 655 Genesee Street, added branch stores and continued operations until the cost of lifetime warranties, a strike by its delivery and warehouse workers and two new chain retailers combined to force the chain to close its five stores and service center in February 1990.

Walter Urbanski and Edward J. Przylucki were other pioneers, originally managing a Firestone automotive store and then opening Lucki-Urban Inc. at 854 Broadway in 1947 as an appliance company. By 1980, the company was known as Lucki-Urban Furniture Inc. at 881 Broadway, with the Lucki-Urban Home & Auto Inc. store. Its slogan was "Home of 4,000 Bargains." It opened a location at 6199 Transit Road in 1988, and in January 1989, the same month Burnham's shut down, it announced the closing of the Broadway store. "People live in the suburbs now"[256] was its response. In February 1990, it ended up shutting down the Transit Road store, leaving its customers with worthless contracts (and a bad taste for lifetime service in their mouths).

WEED & COMPANY AND WALBRIDGE & COMPANY

G. & T. Weed hardware store opened its doors in 1818. This is the White Building in the 1940s, with Weed & Company as one of the tenants. *Courtesy of WNY Heritage Press.*

Two of Buffalo's longest-running firms closed before many of us ever stepped foot through their doorways. These two firms had an interwoven life, bound by their merchandise: hardware.

Buffalo was still an infant in 1818, having just been burned to the ground a few years earlier by the British during the War of 1812 and then only becoming a village of about two thousand persons in 1816. On September 23, 1818, G. & T. Weed opened its doors to the village of Buffalo. It included "a very general and extensive assortment of Hardware, Cutlery, Sadlery, Cabinet Wares & Iron-mongery."[257] George and Thaddeus Weed had ventured from Connecticut and built their first store at 222 Main Street (renumbered 284 in 1869), at the northwest corner of Main and Swan Streets. They were able to stay at that site until about 1898, at which time they moved up the block to 292 Main Street, in the White Building.

In 1827, George bought out Thaddeus, and the firm became George Weed & Company, with Samuel F. Pratt and General Lucius Storrs as partners.[258] That same year, George died, and his partners carried on the business. In 1829, Thaddeus bought back the Weed interest in the business, and it was known as Weed & Pratt. In 1836, Thaddeus again exited the business, and sixteen-year-old Pascal P. Pratt entered the business as a clerk. In 1842, it became S.F. Pratt & Company when Pascal became a partner.

In 1851, Dewitt C. Weed, son of Thaddeus, purchased the business, and it became Dewitt C. Weed & Company. In 1876, his brother, Hobart Weed, took over upon Dewitt's death along with James R. Smith, the firm now being known as Weed & Company. Smith was a member of the lumber firm Smith, Fassett & Company and was involved in other businesses.[259]

"In the early days of its existence, the patronage consisted of as many Indians as whites."[260] The store carried "everything known in American, German and English hardware,"[261] importing goods from Sheffield, England, as well as carrying American brands. The company established both a wholesale and retail trade, opened a warehouse at 95 Swan Street and purchased a Rochester, New York firm in 1910. "For many years after its opening it was the only store of its kind within a day's journey."[262]

In 1844, Parmalee & Hadley opened up a hardware store at 119 Main Street, which the owners continued until 1854, when they moved to 207 Main Street. By 1860, Elijah Hadley took control of the business, the business becoming Hadley & Husted, and moved back to 119 Main Street. Charles C. Nichols was bookkeeper at the time.

In 1868, Nichols joined Hadley in the new firm of Hadley & Nichols at 271 Main Street, and the following year, Charles E. Walbridge purchased the firm. Walbridge had worked for Pratt & Company in the 1850s, later enlisting and taking part in the Civil War. Walbridge returned to work for Pratt & Company after the war and later purchased Hadley & Nichols.[263]

In 1873, he moved to the Sherman block on Washington Street, and in 1879, he built a new store at 297–301 Washington Street. Harry Walbridge and George A. Bell joined the firm in 1884, it becoming known as Walbridge & Company. The company was successful, and it was able to purchase "the entire stock of shelf hardware, and the good will of the firm of Pratt & Company"; Pratt had retired in 1886.[264]

In 1888, the company claimed to "do a larger hardware business than any other house in the State outside of New York City." It added a warehouse at 80 Main Street, a Fillmore Avenue foundry and new quarters at Washington and South Division Streets.[265]

A few years later, in 1891, its building was destroyed by fire. It carried on in a temporary location on Seneca Street, and a new building was erected the same year on the same site. Even this was not enough for the fast-growing concern. It built a new store in 1900 at 392–394 Main Street and added four branch stores in 1915, covering the entire city.

In 1922, the company was incorporated as Walbridge & Company Inc., with a capital stock valued at $3.5 million in today's dollars.[266] The company erected a new office building, designed by Bley & Lyman, at Franklin and Court Streets in September 1924.[267] Something happened along the way,

In 1884, the Walbridge & Company hardware store opened. In September 1924, it constructed this building at Franklin and Court Streets in Buffalo for its flagship store. This photo is circa 1930s. *Author's collection.*

and the business experienced severe growing pains that resulted in a second mortgage on the property and the sudden closing of the business in April 1926. It was immediately sold to Weed & Company.[268] The failure of Walbridge & Company resulted in the foreclosure of the building in November 1926.[269]

Weed & Company celebrated its 125th anniversary in the midst of World War II, and radio announcements urged "Buffalonians to buy War Bonds."[270] The company had retail locations at 292 Main Street and at Main and Genesee Streets, closing the 292 Main location in 1956. "Sentiment rather than profit has been the motive for keeping the store open in recent years," stated Executive Vice-President P.O. Rial.[271] A changing business climate brought about the closing of its last retail store in 1959, leaving just the wholesale outlet at 95 Swan Street.[272]

International Fastener Research Corporation of Los Angeles finally ended the local company's life when it purchased the wholesale business in July 1963. The company, owned by David Weisz,[273] sold the inventory in November, and the wholesale business was merged with International Fastener's operation in Philadelphia.[274]

The former warehouse at 95 Swan Street is still standing.

Year founded: 1818
Year closed: 1963

Victor's Furniture

The size of the estate left by Arthur Victor in 1928 was amazing, even by today's standards, leaving the equivalent of $8.6 million. Where did he amass such wealth?

In 1901, he opened A. Victor & Company at 514 Main Street with Henry Nathan during the Pan-American Exposition. Having worked in Detroit at Peoples Outfitting Company, Victor felt that he knew the furniture business well enough to make a go of it.

In 1927, with business booming, they decided to build a ten-story building at Genesee and Pearl Streets. But before he could see it completed, Victor died in 1927. The building, built on the former Majestic Theater site, was opened in 1928, complete with white terra-cotta front. Henry Nathan, then president, died in 1931, and Arthur Victor Jr. took over, running the business at twenty-nine years of age.[275]

Victor Jr. took the company in new directions, adding men's and women's clothing in the 1930s, toys and, in later years, appliances. In 1956, a New York City investor acquired interests in Victor and Kobacker Furniture Company, with plans to form a chain of furniture stores,[276] but that plan fell through.

In 1968, the company was sold to Dolly Madison, which at the time owned thirty-four retail furniture stores, as well as manufacturing interests,[277] and Victor retired from the company. In the late 1970s, the company began renting furniture as Aarrow Furniture Rental. In the early 1980s, it began a service furnishing corporate housing, and in 1981, the store moved from its longtime spot downtown to the Broadway Market area. The firm was renamed Sherman's, which is part of a four-showroom chain based in Poughkeepsie, New York.[278]

Victor & Company furniture opened in 1901 during the Pan-American Exposition. It was highly successful, and in 1928, it built this ten-story white building. The building was demolished to make room for a hotel. *Courtesy of David Steele.*

The former Victor store on Main Street was later sold and became a Hyatt Hotel, which it still is today. A location at Thruway Mall was open until at least 1995.

Year founded: 1901
Year closed: After 1995

OTHER LOCAL STORES

Furniture stores and factories were once abundant in Buffalo, with ample wood supplies from nearby lumber companies. Michael Berst served an apprenticeship as a cabinetmaker in his home of Germany. "His skill with wood enabled him to pay for his trip to America by serving as a ship's carpenter."[279] He came to Buffalo and began his carpentry business in 1832 in the vicinity of 651 Washington Street. His son, Peter Michael, learned the skill from his father and took over the business in 1880, naming it P.M. Berst.

Over time, the business grew into a general furniture store. In 1884, the business relocated to South Park Avenue, and in 1965, it moved to Seneca Street and Indian Church Road. A fifth-generation family member owned the business, and the store celebrated its 160th anniversary in 1992. It was doing about $1 million in sales, but by 1996, it was no longer listed in the city directory. After a run of 164 years, it appears to have met the fate of nearly all the local businesses of the twentieth century.

Gardner Furniture began in 1919 at 1366 Main Street in Buffalo. A fire in 1968 destroyed the company's warehouse, so it built a new store in Getzville, New York. In 1972, it closed the Main Street store and added a store in Orchard Park in 1978. It purchased several other stores and continued expanding until 1998, when it announced that all locations were shutting down.[280] Just six months later, several former executives of the business opened a new furniture store in the former Orchard Park location of Gardner Furniture. Smith & Schulte Furniture was still in operation in 2007 but was closed by August 2008.

In 1897, Fred Scherer started a furniture store in Buffalo. Scherer sold all types of furniture at its location on an original site on Genesee Street between Oak and Elm Streets in downtown Buffalo. The company was named F. Scherer and Son Furniture after his son Fred joined the business. The senior

In 1895, Household Outfitting opened for business. It was later purchased by Sattler's, becoming Sattler's Home Furnishings stores. This is an early newspaper ad. *Author's collection.*

Fred retired in 1920 and turned the company over to his son. In the 1930s, it moved to its present location at the corner of Genesee and Oak Streets. Junior turned over the business to his brother, Frank, in 1955.[281] When the Kensington Expressway was built, it ended almost at the company's front door.

Most of the other businesses along the street have long since passed. In the 1960s, the company supposedly tore down half its building to accommodate parking. Fred Scherer III took over the company in 1977, and it is still in business today, selling primarily high-quality wood furniture.

Hona Spangenthal and his son, Adolph, founded H. Spangenthal & Company in 1895 at the southwest corner of Huron and Washington Streets, known as Roosevelt Plaza. That same year, Household Outfitting Company Inc., what it would be known as, was listed in the city directory. The store carried furniture, home furnishings and "radio and electrical appliances."[282] In 1939, it moved to larger quarters at 575 Main Street, a remodeled six-story building.[283]

The roots of Stewart & Benson date back to 1847. This was the store at 501 Main Street. The theater is gone, and all of the businesses in this photo have since closed. *Courtesy of David Torke.*

"The store has model rooms which enable a customer to visualize effectively how furniture will look in a home."[284]

By 1945, it had opened a branch and warehouse at 345 Broadway, as well as in the new Thruway Plaza in 1951. In 1957, retiring owner Edwin Spangenthal sold the company to Seneca Warehouse & Industrial Center Inc., which was headed by Irving Levick, who was also chairman of Sattler's. Household became Sattler's Home Furnishings stores, and eventually all the locations were shuttered. The building at 575 Main Street was vacant in 1962.

N. Cooper & Company opened for business in 1847 as a saddlery at 123 Main Street. A few years later, employee Frederick Loegler became owner along with Christian Wolf, another harness maker, and they moved to 360 Main Street. In 1870, Henry Becker joined, and it became Loegler & Becker at 460 Main Street. Henry Becker & Company was the firm name after he took over and moved it to 9 Court Street. One employee was John G. Wickson, who by 1903 was president of the newly named Becker & Wickson Company. Wickson was also president of Mayor Philip Becker's grocery business.

In 1910, J. Fred Stewart was secretary of the company, and in 1914, together with Harry E. Benson, they bought the business and renamed it

Stewart & Benson Inc. The company had a good run selling trunks and leather goods, moving to 501 Main Street in 1959, later opening a travel bureau and moving the leather business to Amherst, New York, in the 1990s and the travel business to Cheektowaga, New York. By 1998, there is no record of the company. The building at 501 was still empty, with the Stewart & Benson sign still visible nine years later. In about 2011, the building was remodeled into apartments.

Catalogue showrooms were once the rage in town. The reason they lasted as long as they did was due to a loophole in state laws that stated that if a manufacturer set a price, a retailer had to sell it at that price.[285] The only ones that didn't have to abide by that were wholesalers, so the catalogue store— basically a wholesaler direct to the public—boomed. Brand Names Sales Inc. was started in Tonawanda, New York, as Hambleton & Carr in 1952, growing to fifteen stores. At the end of its existence in 2001, it still had eleven stores. Century Housewares Inc. was another local catalogue company, headquartered in Orchard Park, New York. By 1973, it had twenty-nine locations,[286] but by the 1980s, the discount department stores had forced the former gift catalogue chain to change directions. The owners opened a discount store called Shoppers' Choice and expanded across the area. They eventually sold that to Big R Distributing, owned by Anthony Ragusa, one of Twin Fair's founders. Century Housewares shuttered its doors in 1983.

Nineteenth-century Buffalo newspaper ads often featured a company known as Irish & English Furniture Store, one that few have probably heard of. It was founded in 1857 by Charles G. Irish, succeeded by his son, John P., in 1876 when he joined Henry English, who ran a local auction house. The furniture store at 303–307 Washington Street handled "the best goods only, and at prices which have never been duplicated elsewhere."[287] It also manufactured "fine parlor and library furniture," as well as sold carpets, house furnishings and bedding. In 1883, it established an installment plan. When English died in 1905, Irish continued the operation until he retired in 1915, at which time he closed the store. It used a lot of newspaper advertising and did "an enormous trade as to be enabled to quote lower prices than ever."[288]

Otto Ulbrich was a bookkeeper in 1870, and the following year, he was in business with Charles Herger as Herger & Ulbrich, stationers, at 365 Main Street. By 1880, he was in business with Spencer S. Kingsley as Ulbrich & Kingsley, and in 1887, he was solo, as "successor to Ulbrich & Kingsley," bookseller and stationer, operating Otto Ulbrich Company.[289] The company suffered several fires in the early years, but none broke Ulbrich's spirit, and he always reopened in a new location, ending up at 386 Main Street in

Lederman's was a popular furniture store located across from the Broadway Market in Buffalo. The Art Deco ornamentation survives to this day. *Photo by author.*

1893. In 1923, he opened a branch on Delaware Avenue and then on West Chippewa Street in 1939.

Ulbrich was a book publisher dating back to at least 1878 and on into the 1940s. In 1964, the company moved to 446 Main Street, as its property was being demolished for the new Main Place Mall. It had five plaza branches and purchased the office supply business of Millington Lockwood Inc. By 1989, the business climate had greatly changed. The flailing company filed for Chapter 11 bankruptcy protection. It had eleven stores by that time and closed several immediately. The company emerged a different one, attempting to fight the chain office stores as Office Plus Inc. That store closed in 1994,[290] leaving its owners bankrupt and deep in debt.[291]

A few other stores worth mentioning include Lederman, Poppenberg's furniture and piano stores, Select and Martin and Hersee furniture store and factory, which was open for ninety-four years before closing in 1930.

Department Stores

My father was the shoe buyer for all shoe departments of AM&A's. Every year we had a picnic in our back yard in Kenmore for all the shoe employees (130–150 people). We had a professional Bingo caller, tons of gifts, plenty of good food and drinks and lots of fun for all!

—anonymous

The department store is the great variety store, the place where many of the memories of downtown or Broadway-Fillmore were born. Whether it's AM&A's, Hens & Kelly, Sattler's or one of the many others, there are many fond memories tied to those now defunct stores.

Unlike other cities, where one store was the dominant one, for many years in Buffalo you could shop at five or more department stores. And the largest of the stores, Sattler's, was located two miles from downtown in the Broadway-Fillmore shopping district. According to former advertising and promotion manager Bob Cornelius, the company had to entice people to the store on a daily basis, and it worked.

Department stores were community leaders. During the world wars, they usually led war bond sales. J.N. Adam had an army exhibit in April 1944, Hengerer's a Norman Rockwell art and bond show in July 1943 and Hens & Kelly a war bond sale in April 1945. The stores sponsored parades and observed national holidays and celebrations. Most, if not all, had Santa Claus at Christmastime, and visiting him became a tradition for thousands of Western New York children. At Barnum's, "Santa Claus has made his headquarters there ever since S.O. Barnum arrived in Buffalo." J.N. Adam sponsored the annual Santa arrival, dating at least to 1939, and the celebration at Civic Stadium drew families from far and wide. In 1946, twenty thousand people jammed the stadium to see the arrival of Santa and his cadre of guests. The Hengerer's Santa was also on local television.

The Broadway-Fillmore business district held Christmas parades starting in 1947, sponsored by Sattler's. The 1953 parade attracted 200,000 people to see Santa and then fill the stores for a day of shopping.

E.W. Edwards held the Sue Hasting Marionette Show during the 1943 holiday season.

Over time, the store window displays became more elaborate and more important in selling merchandise, but at Christmas, they were a wonderland of visual entertainment. In 1969, AM&A's featured "the greatest windows ever shown in this country." They had been used one year by B. Altman in New York City and purchased by AM&A's for display in Buffalo.

According to Jan Whitaker in her book *Service and Style*, department stores were important in many ways, including as exhibitors of museum-quality displays. J.N. Adam held a Polish exhibit in July 1943, AM&A's an aerospace exhibit in August 1965 and Sattler's a Polish festival in June 1963. In 1965, Sattler's displayed a seven- by fifteen-foot Easter egg at 998 Broadway. Kleinhans also tried to lure customers with a jewel exhibition in November 1953.

Whitaker also wrote that the department store was important in dictating fashion styles to the middle class, more so after World War II. Stores held fashion shows, etiquette classes, music and dance lessons and much more. J.N. Adam held fashion shows at least as early as January 1942, AM&A's held shows in its restaurant and Sattler's held diet workshops in the 1960s.

Since shopping was then considered a woman's chore, most stores didn't try to attract male shoppers until later years. Tearooms were designed for ladies to stop in after a day of shopping, and Miss Vincent's and Mary Burns were just two of the tearooms in Buffalo stores. As the shopping experience changed, so did the tearooms. Many gave way to restaurants for the whole family or were just abandoned. That elusive male shopper was soon being courted because he was considered less fussy and rarely returned anything. J.N. Adam opened the "Stag Club" in 1950, hoping to lure male shoppers.

The stores faced many issues over time, including women's rights, pay inequities, race relations and overall employment issues. Most stores did not employ women as clerks until the twentieth century, overtime pay was unheard of and child labor was common.

In Buffalo, the stores tried to circumvent trouble by offering insurance and employee lounges and raising pay. Sattler's published the monthly *Sattlerite* newsletter highlighting employee accomplishments, and in 1942, it added a pension plan. In 1947, J.N. Adam increased the pay of clerks and hired a training director, and in 1949, it added employee insurance. Hengerer's opened general employment offices in October 1943, and Hens & Kelly let female employees run the store for two days in October 1939.

Department stores were usually the first places someone rode an elevator or escalator, the former with well-dressed operators wearing white gloves and hats. The first escalators in Buffalo were said to be installed in J.N. Adam or possibly Hens & Kelly, which claimed a 1920s installation. Many stores also added public telephones, possibly the first their customers had used. The stores developed additional community goodwill by sponsoring clubs and opening rooms for community groups.

In about 1910, AM&A's and Hengerer's sponsored company football teams, prior to the formation of the National Football League.[292] AM&A's also had a mutual aid association, dating back to the 1930s, and a store choir. Hengerer's opened a youth center on the sixth floor in August 1942. The stores also allowed community groups to "run" the store and collect profits for their organizations. AM&A's worked with the Junior League as far back as the 1930s and maybe earlier, and Hengerer's worked with Millard Fillmore Hospital in the 1930s.

During the Great Depression, the department stores tried to instill confidence in the citizens by sponsoring Buffalo Day, and many of them invested in their buildings, providing jobs and purchasing local materials. They invited educational, sports, music, movie and television personalities to their stores. This was free entertainment for the citizens at a time when money for entertainment was scarce. At the same time, it brought people into the stores, some of whom would purchase goods or return when they did have the money.

By 1959, there were fifteen suburban shopping centers in the Buffalo area, and to stay competitive, the department stores started opening branches in those plazas. The department stores also found a way to pool their resources by operating a delivery service, which was started in January 1940. Seven downtown department stores began the joint delivery venture under the auspices of Downtown Merchants Delivery Company Inc. The service would make two deliveries a day to Buffalo and Kenmore and one to select suburban areas. "The delivery fleet will consist of 60 trucks" and "a maximum capacity of about 50,000 packages (a day) during peak season."[293]

One of Buffalo's biggest department stores started as Adam, Meldrum & Company, prior to Anderson joining the partnership. This is circa 1874. *Courtesy of Buffalo State College Archives, Courier-Express Collection.*

The stores included Hengerer's, Hens & Kelly, J.N. Adam, E.W. Edwards & Son, Flint & Kent, L.L. Berger and Oppenheim, Collins & Company. "By joining forces we are able to put into effect the most modern and efficient methods," stated Winthrop Kent, president of Flint & Kent.[294] Buffalo's biggest department store, AM&A's, joined the organization in September 1941 as a way to prevent duplication and save gas, especially during the war years.[295]

The first location of the business was at 101–107 Elm Street, later moving to a four-story, 360,000-square-foot building at 255 Great Arrow Drive. The delivery service operated until 1981.

Eventually, all the stores would leave the city for good. A few are still in business under different names, but downtown and Broadway-Fillmore have never been the same since.

ADAM, MELDRUM & ANDERSON (AM&A's)

Perhaps Buffalo's best-known, or most beloved, department store was Adam, Meldrum & Anderson, better known as AM&A's. It was one of the few stores that stayed locally owned until it was sold, and it still survives under the Bon-Ton banner.

Robert Borthwick Adam was born in Peebles, Scotland, in 1833, leaving school at a young age to begin working. In 1857, he arrived in the United States and was immediately offered a job with Boston retailer Hogg, Brown and Taylor, leading merchants and fellow Scottish countrymen.[296]

When Adam was ready to embark on his own, he probably traveled down the Erie Canal to the bustling city of Buffalo, where he joined Herbert A. Meldrum and Alexander Whiting to form Adam, Meldrum & Whiting dry goods store. They opened for business on March 21, 1867, at 308 and 310 Main Street,[297] known as the American Block, in the former American Hotel, "from whose balcony Abraham Lincoln in 1861, had delivered one of his most celebrated addresses."[298] The first store "was modest in size, 22 feet wide and 85 feet deep."[299] It "was open from 8 A.M. to 8 P.M. and its 11 employees sold $77 [$1,170] worth of products."[300] A modest beginning for the store.

By 1871, it was bursting at the seams, and it doubled in size. Whiting left the company in 1872, and it became known as Adam & Meldrum, "Importers, Jobbers and Retailers"[301] located at 396, 398, 400 and 402 Main Street. Then, in 1874, the founders decided to expand their offerings and become a department store. That same year, they again enlarged the building and not long afterward took up the entire American Block in a building five stories high and almost two hundred feet long.

In 1876, William Anderson joined the ranks, and the name was changed to Adam, Meldrum & Anderson, the name that would stand for more than one hundred years. The business slowly blossomed, and by 1888, the company had made eight enlargements to its building.[302]

In 1886, Buffalonians were part of a world first. Westinghouse Electric Company had been formed that year and built the "first successful alternating current generating plant"[303] in Buffalo, with Adam, Meldrum & Anderson Company the pioneer user.[304] Company cofounder Robert Adam reminisced wistfully in his later years, "We installed the first electric lighting system in Buffalo. No other scene, during the multiplying years, remains so distinctly in my memory as the first lighting of this store by electricity."[305]

After company cofounder Herbert Meldrum died in 1891, the company was incorporated with $400,000 ($9.89 million) in capital stock in February 1892. It joined the Syndicate Trading Company (known as the "Scottish Syndicate") before 1896, it being a joint purchasing company organized with eleven other Scottish dry goods stores across the country, with a buying office in New York City.[306] The last man to join the company, William Anderson, died in 1897.

In March 1903, the company purchased four properties on Pearl Street, with plans to level them and add an eight-story addition to its store.

Robert Adam, the man behind the great growth of AM&A's, died in 1904. His nephew, Robert B. Scott, had come to America, and Adam, who was childless, adopted and raised him, changing his name to Robert B. Adam II.[307] Adam II took over as president of the company, taking it to the next level under his stewardship.[308]

By 1907, it was again looking to grow and added two additional elevators, giving it a total of eight and the most floor space between New York City and Chicago. AM&A's was a hit.

AM&A's opened the Adam, Meldrum & Anderson State Bank, and by 1925, it had thirteen thousand depositors.[309] Robert Adam II, along with guiding AM&A's into the twentieth century, was a collector of eighteenth-century literature, the collection being started by his father. The AM&A's Bank turned out to be a tremendous drain on the company's resources, and with Adam's manuscript collection used as collateral, the collection was sold to private collectors to pay back creditors. In 1956, AM&A's finally sold the troubled bank to Manufacturers & Traders Trust Company.

In 1924, AM&A's embarked on the erection of a seven-story building that extended from Main Street to Pearl Street and added seventy thousand square feet to the original store. By then, "AM&A's had become so much of an institution in Buffalo's business activities and family life."[310] The building expansion allowed many departments to enlarge, including rug and carpets, which occupied one whole floor; ready-to-wear clothing also occupied a floor, and china/glassware and furniture occupied two floors. They also added public conveniences such as waiting rooms, telephone booths and writing rooms.[311] This "annex" cost $500,000 ($6.38 million) and was opened in April 1925 to much fanfare at 404 Main Street.[312]

In November 1932, the company purchased the J.L. Hudson men's store at 410 Main Street, adjacent to its building. The $350,000 ($5.59 million) price included the stock, building and name. The purchase allowed AM&A's to broaden its clothing line but still keep the popular Hudson name. It also gave "the company the largest Main Street frontage of any Buffalo store."[313] J.L. Hudson Jr., manager of the store, stayed on with AM&A's.

Robert Adam II died in April 1940, followed in August by his wife, who had briefly taken over as company president. In 1942, twenty-four-year-old Robert B. Adam III took over as company president. He served in the military during World War II and returned to his position with the company after his service was complete.

Adam said that he originally had no plans to join the company started by his grandfather. As a child, he had seen it lose money during the Great Depression and watched as the bank collapsed and his father's manuscript collection was sold. After his parents died, he found himself the majority shareholder of the business and immediately worked to try and right the struggling company. With "some old pros," he was able to turn things around.[314] Under the stewardship of Robert Adam III, AM&A's would not lose money until after his retirement many years later.

With World War II over, AM&A's put a new façade on the store, the first it ever had. A granite and glass front, extending from 404 Main Street to 410 Main Street, gave it 185 feet of frontage. Buffalo's Duane Lyman & Associates were the architects of the 1947 work. Included in the update was a new sign in gold-leaf letters in granite that replaced the original sign.[315]

Two months later, the company announced the opening of its first branch store at the University Plaza on Main Street near the University at Buffalo. The five-thousand-square-foot store was designed to be expandable. Adam noted that "our purpose in establishing this branch in University Plaza is for the sake of public convenience—principally for the people in the North Buffalo, Kenmore, Tonawanda and Amherst areas."[316] This was where the population was growing, so the store wanted to be close to those neighborhoods.

Sometime during the 1940s, AM&A's began the annual tradition that only ended when the downtown store finally closed. The store filled its Main Street windows with "a wonderland of animated figures" at Christmastime. As time went on, more Victorian figures were added until "hundreds of pieces of equipment" were part of the special display. Tens of thousands of people would make the trip downtown to view the wondrous display while doing their holiday shopping, and even years later, many would bring their children and grandchildren to see the displays.[317]

AM&A's continued its growth by opening branches in the Sheridan Plaza in Tonawanda and Airport Plaza in Cheektowaga. When E.W. Edwards & Son pulled out of the Buffalo market, AM&A's took over its store in the L.B. Smith Plaza on Abbott Road in Lackawanna in October 1952.

In late 1959, J.N. Adam & Company (located directly across the street) announced that it would be closing its doors forever in 1960. AM&A's seized on the opportunity and decided to move into the building. "Due to the growth and expansion of our business...we for some time have been aware of the need for more adequate space and facilities in the downtown area so that we might better serve our customers."[318]

Adam also believed that construction of the New York State Thruway would bring more people to the downtown store, and "more than 8 acres of floor space completely renovated" would highlight the move.[319] Showing its faith, AM&A's signed a fifty-year lease on the building. The company at that time had 1,950 employees, 900 working at the downtown store.

After seven months of remodeling the former J.N. store, which was "stripped back to the bare walls and rebuilt," it was finished with the most modern of retailing adornment, lighting and fixtures. New elevators, air conditioning and a new restaurant on the eighth floor, the Yankee Doodle Room, were added. Local radio station WBEN broadcast its lunch hour show from there. At the end of business on Wednesday, July 27, 1960, it closed the doors at 404 Main Street, and for two days, workers carted stock across the street to the new store.

In what was probably one of the most interesting store moves in Buffalo history, Main Street was closed to traffic on Monday, August 1, 1960. A red carpet was laid across the street, and "to the stirring music of bagpipes played by the Scottish Highlanders, AM&A's 2,200 store associates marched four abreast out of the old store [across the street] and into the new store."[320] It must have been quite a scene.

The company continued its growth in 1961, when it opened a new eighteen-thousand-square-foot store in the Southgate Plaza in West Seneca. In mid-July 1963, a group of businessmen called Backers Realty Inc. pushed for redevelopment of the former AM&A's building and adjacent property.

The directors of Backers included the presidents of Kleinhans, Victor's, AM&A's, H.D. Taylor, Barcalo, Hengerer's, Erie County Savings Bank (which was erecting a new headquarters at Main and Church Streets), Liberty National Bank (which was located at the other end of the block at Main and Court Streets) and Denton, Cottier & Daniels.[321] One stumbling block of the redevelopment was that AM&A's still had a lease on its former store, which didn't expire until May 1, 1964.[322]

In April 1964, just three years after opening, it enlarged the Southgate Plaza store, which was then 100,000 square feet in size.[323] In August of that same year, its former store on Main Street downtown was sold, and

This is the AM&A's building in 1976 in the former J.N. Adam store. The Brisbane building (Woolworth's and Kleinhans) is to the left, or north, of AM&A's. *Courtesy of Buffalo State College Archives,* Courier-Express *Collection.*

the construction of the Main Place Mall began. Liberty National Bank purchased the former J.L. Hudson store at 410 Main Street, which was adjacent to its building.[324]

Just two months later, AM&A's purchased several buildings on Eagle Street, between Washington and Ellicott Streets, where a "new service and warehouse building" would be erected. The downtown store, in 1964, accounted "for about 50 percent of AM&A's sales volume."[325] The new building would "adjoin the company's present service building at the northeast corner of Washington and Eagle."[326]

In March 1966, AM&A's announced plans to again remodel the downtown store, which would coincide with the opening of the new Main Place Mall across the street and its 100th anniversary.[327] It also opened an expanded Thruway Plaza store that year.[328] The company was proud to celebrate its anniversary in 1967, and a plaque commemorating the event was placed on the building that September.[329]

In order to make access to its warehouse facility on Washington Street easier, especially during inclement weather, the company asked for and received approval from the city in 1969 to build a bridge connecting the store and warehouse.[330] Apparently, that was never constructed, but it did build a large, dark, "super creepy" tunnel that ran under Washington Street between the buildings.[331]

That year also saw the opening of a home furnishing store,[332] 1970 saw a remodeled Thruway Plaza store,[333] 1971 saw an expanded Southgate Plaza store[334] and the closing of the Abbott Road store[335] and 1972 saw a store added in the Eastern Hills Mall.[336]

A new eighty-two-thousand-square-foot store was opened in the Lockport Mall in September 1974, making for its seventh store.[337] In 1976, it completed a $300,000 ($1.15 million) renovation of the flagship downtown store, which would prove to be its last.[338]

In 1980, Bob Adam's son-in-law, J. Keith Alford, was named president of the firm. Adam himself continued as chairman and chief executive officer until April 1989, when he stepped down as CEO at seventy years of age. Alford took over the company's presidency. Adam was proud of the fact that the chain had not "reported a loss since he got there four decades ago,"[339] a feat of which any company would be proud. The company's sales probably peaked about 1988, when it reached $132.5 million ($244 million),[340] but there were big changes on the horizon.

In February 1990, AM&A's made a business decision that most of Buffalo's other retailers were making or had already made: it agreed to move into the area's largest and newest mall, the Walden Galleria, just a mile from its store at the Thruway Mall, which was an anchor. The Thruway Mall store was closed, and AM&A's was subsequently sued, but it continued the move into the former B. Altman store in the Galleria.[341]

In August 1993, the former Yankee Doodle Room restaurant in the Main Street store was taken over by Vito's Gourmet Market and Deli, a new "yuppie" attraction.[342] The move would prove to be fatal to Vito's, which had agreed to open in several AM&A's stores.

Bob Adam III died in September 1993 at seventy-five years old.[343] Almost immediately, rumors of the sale of the company began to swirl around town. His widow died in April 1994, and the rumors became more intense. The Bon-Ton Stores Inc. of York, Pennsylvania, acknowledged that it was interested in AM&A's, but company CEO J. Keith Alford, who had always been upfront and available to the media, suddenly became unresponsive and did not return calls. Therefore, news outlets took that as an imminent sign.[344]

When Bob Adam had stepped down in 1989, it was a profitable company. Three years later, it was losing money, and some analysts said that it was because it didn't "define its niche as young and affluent shoppers moved to other stores."[345] The early 1990s recession may have hit the company harder than expected, and Alford fired three top executives in early 1994.

University at Buffalo professor Arun K. Jain said at the time, "If they sell now, they'll be remembered in a positive way."[346] He felt that if they waited, the company might have shut down or would have lost even more value.

On May 17, 1994, the news everyone feared finally broke. The Bon-Ton had agreed to buy the chain for $2.1 million in cash and assume $40 million in debt and other liabilities.[347] The sale was completed in July 1994.[348]

When Bon-Ton purchased the chain, it had ten locations, and questions about whether the flagship downtown store would stay open were asked. Just a few months into its stewardship, Bon-Ton realized that the downtown store was bigger than it needed, so it closed one floor and spent $200,000 on a minor cosmetic makeover to the store.[349]

The AM&A's distribution center on Kenmore Avenue (there since moving from Great Arrow Avenue ten years earlier) was closed in February 1995.[350] A few weeks later, Bon-Ton did what many hoped it wouldn't: it announced the closing of the downtown store. The store was losing an estimated $5,000 a day, according to Bon-Ton chairman and CEO Tim Grumbacher. "We internally explored various potential alternatives, including downsizing and tax relief. However, we simply could not realize sufficient savings to offset the projected $1.7 million loss that we would have sustained had we kept the downtown store open."

People have to remember that AM&A's sold because it was failing, and a big part of its problem was the downtown store.[351] Community and political leaders were upset at the sudden decision, and many predicted the further decline of downtown, already balancing precariously near the edge, after AM&A's closed. The exit from downtown was less than spectacular. There wasn't a big closing sale, and employees complained that Bon-Ton didn't really try to help them find new employment, while Bon-Ton maintained that it did its best.

No matter what really happened, on March 19, 1995, the last vestige of Buffalo retailing, dating back 128 years, was put to sleep for good. The building signs were taken down the next day.[352] Downtown would continue to suffer, and it would be years before it would start to recover. Vito's Market, which had opened in several AM&A's stores, went bankrupt and closed.

Businessman Richard Taylor of Toronto, Canada, attempted to resurrect the grand store by opening an upscale ladies' department store in 1998. The store's high-priced selection and initial policies (such as no sneakers; only heels in the store) proved to be too narrow for downtown's shopping clientèle, and after an eight-month run, the store closed its doors, leaving the massive building empty.[353]

In 2006, the Walden Galleria Bon-Ton location closed, and in 2007, the Northtown Plaza location closed as well. The Sheridan Plaza, Southgate Plaza, Eastern Hills Mall, Lockport Mall, Summit Park Mall, Olean Mall and McKinley Mall locations are still open.

A new owner proposed plans to convert the building in 2007 to retail, residential and commercial space, but that fell through. New owners have attempted to reuse the building, and preservationists successfully had the property, known as the J.N. Adam–AM&A Historic District, listed on the National Register of Historic Places in 2009.

Year founded: 1867
Year closed: 1994 (still open as the Bon-Ton)

J.N. Adam (J.N.'s)

Robert B. Adam arrived in Buffalo in 1867 and soon after was operating one of Buffalo's favorite dry goods stores, Adam, Meldrum & Company. He contacted his brother, James Noble Adam, back in their homeland of Scotland and "induced him to visit him in Buffalo."[354]

James Noble, or J.N., came to the United States and settled in New Haven, Connecticut, where he established a dry goods business that he operated for seven years. He returned to Buffalo and opened J.N. Adam & Company with local businessman William H. Hotchkiss on October 20, 1881, at 292 Main Street, in the White Building. "The business was founded on a principle that honesty is the best policy. J.N. would not allow any false statement to be made regarding merchandise, and every advertisement was carefully checked by him."[355]

Business increased, and within ten years, 29 Erie Street and then 92 Pearl Street were added to the store. About ten years later, the company purchased the Stevenson building on Main Street and erected a new store. As business continued to grow, it added two other buildings on each side of it. The buildings were lit and heated by gas. In 1891, it added one telephone, and "in October 1881 the United States Electric Lighting Company gave a lighting exhibition in a factory building at 296 Washington Street and installed ten lamps in the J.N. Adams [*sic*] store in November."[356] At that time, it was "the largest plant in the world running arc lights from incandescent current." It was quite the attraction, and many passersby stopped to view the machinery.[357]

In 1899, Adam and Hotchkiss purchased property on Delaware Avenue and Chippewa Street, and rumors circulated that they were planning to build a new store there, but the store never materialized.

In 1895, Adam was convinced to run for city councilman, which he did and won. He was reelected to a second term. In 1901, Adam was elected alderman of the Twenty-fourth Ward in Buffalo.[358] Hotchkiss, who became president of J.N.'s, was always looking for new investments, and in March 1905, he purchased the William Hengerer Company from its ailing founder with the intention of running both stores independently—or so he intimated.[359]

Just a few weeks later, the two stores were sold as a package deal to John Claflin of H.B. Claflin & Company of New York City on April 13, 1905. Claflin formed the United Dry Goods Companies, which was a $51 million ($1.3 billion) company and would later include Lord & Taylor.[360] In December 1915, a new company was formed, and the stock of United was exchanged for Associated Dry Goods Corporation.[361]

J.N. Adam retired from active business and in November 1905 was elected mayor of Buffalo. He served from 1906 to 1909.[362]

Hengerer's and J.N.'s operated independently, and in 1909, J.N.'s planned a five-story addition, with the razing of the adjacent McArthur building. In 1924, it purchased the Williams block for $1.2 million ($29.7 million), and with that purchase, it owned all the Main Street property from the Brisbane Building to Eagle Street, a total of 350,000 square feet.

By 1926, J.N.'s had 1,200 employees, fifty-six delivery trucks and twenty-six delivery horses. It covered one thousand square miles a day doing "rural" deliveries to Depew, Orchard Park, Williamsville and, in the summer, Derby, Wanakah and Angola on the Lake.[363] The company always tried to accommodate its employees by shortening the workday and providing a hospital, a library and a training department, all on premises.[364]

The company planned its most ambitious modernization in 1935, set to cost $700,000 ($11.1 million). "The persistent increase in the sales and transactions of the past several years has made it necessary to expand all of our selling departments," stated Walter J. Brunmark, president of the concern.[365]

The parent company of J.N's proposed this 1946 remodel of the store, which was later completed. *Courtesy of Buffalo State College Archives,* Courier-Express *Collection.*

A new six-story building, a new façade of "honed-finished, yellow Kasota Vein stone," new elevators and escalators and other modernizations were incorporated.[366] Construction continued until 1939, when the project was completed. In August 1937, it opened a store in Niagara Falls at 114–120 Falls Street.

Business boomed, and the company planned a three-story addition and a ten-story building at Washington and Eagle Streets as postwar building resumed in 1945.[367] By January 1946, it had expanded the plans, and instead, a twelve-story building, a four-story addition, a helicopter pad and a television beacon would be erected.[368] "There will not be a store in America that will be so far advanced at the time this is completed," stated company president Albin O. Holder. There would be over 600,000 square feet of space in the buildings. The $4 million ($44.6 million) expansion was completed in February 1948, and the modern store also included a bakery and a candy shop.

As all the department stores did throughout the years, J.N. Adam sponsored many community events, including Spanish lessons over the radio, opera programs, golf tournaments and Albright Art School sponsorships.[369] It also established five scholarships at University at Buffalo in 1943.[370] In 1949, it provided "health, accident, sickness and death insurance" to its employees.[371]

J.N.'s celebrated its seventy-fifth anniversary in 1956, which would be the last major one it would celebrate. In October 1959, Associated Dry Goods Corporation announced that it would be closing J.N. Adam & Company, and Adam, Meldrum & Anderson would be moving across the street into its building.[372] Associated's other local store, Hengerer's, would remain open. It couldn't justify operating two separate stores on the same street, let alone in the same city.

J.N.'s closed its doors forever, one day earlier than anticipated, having sold out of its stock. In early August 1960, AM&A's marched across the street in a big ceremony to occupy the store. In July 1986, Associated Dry Goods Corporation merged with May Department Stores.[373]

Year founded: 1881
Year closed: 1960

ECKHARDT'S

John H. Eckhardt was known as the "Father of the Broadway-Fillmore business district."[374] He and his wife, Kate L., started John H. Eckhardt Inc. as a dry goods store in about 1891 on the corner of Broadway and Fillmore Avenue on Buffalo's East Side. The store grew quickly and expanded over the years.

In 1920, the Eckhardts retired from active business and leased the store to other operators, including the Boston Store, which was owned by Kobacker's. In 1939, the Eckhardts, restless with retirement, canceled the lease and closed the Boston Store. They demolished the building and constructed a modern store at the same location at a cost of $300,000 ($4.71 million), designed by the local firm of Bley & Lyman. The store contained "continuous windows, with metal sash, to give a modernistic appearance to the structure."[375] It is often compared to, or confused with, the W.T. Grant store, which was located on Main Street in downtown Buffalo.

Mrs. Eckhardt died in May 1941 and John the following month. Their daughter, Alice E. Becker, and grandson, Deon E. Becker, sold the store, merchandise and all the fixtures to Goldblatt's Stores of Chicago in September 1941. On December 7, 1941, the day Pearl Harbor was attacked, Goldblatt's Department Store opened.

On November 27, 1948, the store was closed after employees attempted to unionize and the company refused to acknowledge it, although the company never admitted so. In about 1949, Sears took over the building at 950 Broadway and remained there until 1957. The beautifully designed building is still standing and was converted to office use by the New York State Department of Labor, which had offices in the building from 1959 until the early 1990s.

When the Eckhardts died, they left an estate valued at approximately $482,000 ($7.14 million). The building was owned by family members for decades, and the current owners have kept the building in good condition while they search for a new tenant.

Year founded: 1891, closed 1920
Year reopened: 1940, then closed in 1941 after the owners died

ERION'S

Frederick Erion was born in Germany in 1850, eventually ending up in Buffalo in 1870. After moving away for several years and working several different jobs, he returned, formed a partnership with his brother, John, in 1877 and opened F. Erion & Company Inc., a dry goods store at 509 William Street near Emslie Street, "carrying a general line of dry goods and fancy articles."[376]

By 1880, Erion's had outgrown its location and moved to a larger building at 537 William Street. Another relative, Jacob Erion, had a music store at 543 William Street. The partnership continued until 1883, when John left. He started a lumber and dry goods business at 509 William Street, and Frederick continued the original store until 1903, when he moved the business to 1021–1027 Broadway at Lombard Street. Broadway was known as a thrifty shopping district and was the largest shopping district outside downtown Buffalo. In the 100,000-square-foot department store, "Mr. Erion has carried out many new and original ideas which have been copied by metropolitan stores."[377] He believed in "utmost courtesy to the public and his employees are trained in this attitude toward every customer who visits the store."[378]

The company kept the store at 509 William Street and opened the Erion Piano Company, a music and piano store, in 1903. It "was one of the largest dealers in that section of Buffalo for many years in pianos, victrolas and all

The Erion Piano Company on William Street was an offshoot of the Erion's Department Store. It became a large dealer in instruments and survived more than thirty years before closing. This building is still standing, with some inventive remodeling done over the years. *Photo by author.*

musical instruments."[379] The company celebrated fifty years in business in 1927. In December 1928, Mr. Erion died, and his sons continued operation of the company.

By 1930, Erion Piano Company had moved into the same building as its sister store, and by 1935, the company was closed. The furniture department moved to 760 Fillmore Avenue and operated as Erion Furniture Company until 1954. Jahraus-Braun Company occupied the Broadway store from 1939 until 1951, and Sattler's Annex was the tenant in 1957.

Year founded: 1877
Year closed: 1935

FLINT & KENT

Benjamin Fitch opened a dry goods store at 288 Main Street in 1832, the year Buffalo was incorporated as a city. He also had a clothing store at the corner of Main and Seneca Streets. "At that time lower Main Street was the heart of Buffalo's business section,"[380] close to the docks and busy Erie Canal.

With the addition of partners in 1836, the firm became Fitch, Marvin & Company, located at 140 Main Street. One of his employees was Ethan H. Howard, who became a partner in 1844, the firm then becoming Fitch & Howard. Benjamin Fitch retired in 1853, and with the addition of J.M. Whitcomb, the business was known as Howard, Whitcomb and Company. William B. Flint joined the firm, then located at 207 Main Street.

Henry M. Kent and R.P. Stone joined the firm on February 17, 1865, while Howard and Whitcomb retired, and it became Flint, Kent & Stone (successors to Howard, Whitcomb and Company). Then, in October 1866, Stone sold his interest in the business to Henry C. Howard (the son of Ethan Howard), and it was renamed Flint, Kent & Howard. Just two years later, Howard left due to illness, and the partnership known as Flint & Kent, located at 261 Main Street, was born.

The business continued its growth, moving to larger quarters at 554 Main Street in 1897. The design work for the new store was done by architect Edward Kent, Mr. Kent's son (in 1912, Edward perished on the doomed ship *Titanic*).[381]

The business was incorporated in 1909. The store's original success was in dry goods, but as the city grew, so did Flint & Kent, changing into "ready-to-wear clothing for all occasions."[382] By 1932, the store had four floors of merchandise, "with 46 departments, each of them larger than the original store."[383] The company celebrated its 100th anniversary in 1932, the first anniversary it ever celebrated. Things began to change in 1954 as the store was sold to Charles Jack Hahn, whose father owned Sattler's. Winthrop Kent, one of the previous owners and manager of the store, was retained after the transaction. Hahn expected to make no major changes but planned on updating the store's appearance.

All good things come to an end, and in 1956, Hahn sold the business to another Buffalo upscale clothing store, Sample Inc., which occupied the store until 1959.[384] Huron Stores Inc. took over the premises, and three years later, it fell behind on its obligations and went bankrupt. The store was closed and left empty until 1964, when the building was sold. In 1965, the W.T. Grant store leased the first floor, and the following year, it occupied it as part of an expansion of its adjacent store.[385]

Benjamin Fitch, the original founder, had gone on to be a noted New York City philanthropist. In 1881, he left money and a house on Swan Street in Buffalo to the Charity Organization of Buffalo and endowed the Fitch Creche to be located in the house. It is believed to be the first nursery and day care in the United States.

Year founded: 1832
Year closed: 1956

H.A. MELDRUM, THE ANDERSON COMPANY AND THE SWEENEY STORE

Children do not always wish to follow in the footsteps of their parents. Others do follow into the family business, but being the son of a successful merchant does not guarantee success, nor does it spell imminent failure. The Anderson and Meldrum boys, though, thought that they could duplicate their fathers' business prosperity.

Frank M. Hoffman began his retailing career as a salesman, and later buyer, at AM&A's in the 1880s. He opened his own store, the Hoffman, in 1896 with partners John F. Sweeney, Rudolph Schelbach and Peter McLaren at 460 Main Street, an address that has seen many of Buffalo's retailers.[386]

Herbert Alexander Meldrum was reared in the department store business as the son of Alexander Meldrum of Adam, Meldrum & Anderson. He worked at AM&A's until 1897, at which time he purchased the stock of the Hoffman and formed H.A. Meldrum Company department store with Hoffman and Sweeney.[387]

Meldrum was somewhat of an innovator in Buffalo retailing.

Herbert A. Meldrum was the son of Alexander Meldrum of AM&A's. He opened his own store at 460 Main Street in 1897. This is the store about 1908. *Author's collection.*

This is a great postcard from the Sweeney Store, which opened at 268 Main Street in 1904 after William Hengerer moved to a new location. Chauncey Hamlin would later become president of the concern. *Courtesy of William Bird.*

In 1898, he introduced "the first automobile delivery car in Buffalo. It was a Waverly electric and traversed the streets of Buffalo years before the large commercial houses of the country adopted automobiles for delivery purposes."[388] He also took the first known aerial photo of Buffalo in 1906 as part of a publicity stunt.

The business appeared to do well until it went insolvent in 1922. It is possible that the drain from World War I eventually took a toll on the company. The store assets and building were sold to E.W. Edwards & Son, which took over the store. Meldrum later opened the Meldrum-Hosmer Company Inc. furniture store at 1435 Jefferson Avenue but closed it in 1929. Frank Hoffman died in 1929.

Charles T. and his brother, William R. Anderson, were sons of another of the founders of Adam, Meldrum & Anderson. Having worked in their father's business for years, they left when he died in 1897, the same year Meldrum left. The following year, they were working at the H.A. Meldrum Company store. In May 1900, they opened the Anderson Company department store at 534 Main at Huron Street.

They realized that the building did not suit their needs as built, and in 1901, they remodeled the entrances to the building. "The Huron Street side of the Anderson Company's store is practically one unbroken range of show windows from Main to Pearl streets, an advantage enjoyed by only one other store in Buffalo, H. Kleinhans & Company."[389] The store was open until January 1905, when large advertisements in the local newspapers proclaimed a liquidation sale by the Anderson Company.

During Herbert Meldrum's heyday in 1904, he partnered with John F. Sweeney and William Hamlin to occupy the store that William Hengerer Company was vacating at 268 Main Street and open the Sweeney Company department store.[390] Charles Anderson also joined the firm. The company spent the equivalent of $2 million in today's dollars to renovate the building and was funded with the equivalent of $17 million. Sweeney was the president of the concern, which appears to have succeeded for nine years, when Chauncey J. Hamlin became president. (Actor Harry Hamlin is the grandson of Hamlin.) Sweeney retired from the business in about 1908 and died in January 1913.[391]

The Sweeney Company experienced a strike by its delivery drivers and store clerks in May 1913. On May 7, 1913, the store announced new changes to employee policies:

- *An eight hour day—8.30 a.m. to 5.30 p.m.*
- *The payment of a minimum wage—$5.00 a week for boys—$6.00 a week for women—$12.00 a week for men—$15.00 a week for drivers.*
- *Increased salaries dependent upon efficiency.*
- *An opportunity for all salespeople, in addition to their salaries, to share in a percentage of the increased sales of the store.*
- *Half holidays during July and August.*
- *Vacations with pay.*
- *The establishment of a co-operative association of all the employees.*[392]

These progressive changes (the typical workday was nine hours) brought the striking drivers back to work just days later. The Sweeney Company eased out of existence just months later, when it was announced that it was closing in October 1913 and Hamlin's was taking over its location.[393]

Hamlin's Incorporated was run by Chauncey Hamlin as a bargain store. In early November 1916, the company announced that Hamlin was retiring and closing the business.[394] In the end, with all the business acumen and inherited knowledge they received, nothing guaranteed their ability to operate a successful department store in Buffalo.

The H.A. Meldrum building at 460 Main Street extends through to 271 Pearl Street. It was listed on the National Register of Historic Places in April 2013 and has been remodeled into loft-style apartments. On the Pearl Street side, you can still see the fading "DEPARTMENT STORE DRUM COMPANY" sign at the top of the building.

Year founded: 1896
Year closed: 1913

HENS & KELLY

The story of the Hens & Kelly company starts with another defunct dry goods firm in downtown Buffalo. The proprietor of that establishment, Jeremiah F. Sheehan, was manager at E. Kiannane, a dry goods store at 485 Main Street in 1879. The next year, John J. Kraus started as a salesman for Arend & Morgan, located at 259 Main Street. In 1882, they partnered and opened Kraus & Sheehan at 446 Main Street.

By 1887, Sheehan had left the partnership to work with Edward O'Keefe at J.F. Sheehan & Company, at 485–487 Main Street at the corner of Mohawk, while Kraus stayed at 446 Main Street as John Kraus & Son. In June 1888, O'Keefe resigned for health reasons, and Sheehan continued the business.

Mathias J. Hens was born in Germany, moving to Buffalo in about 1871.[395] After attending Canisius College, he began working for Kraus & Sheehan as a bookkeeper. Legend has it that on a buying trip to New York City in 1883, he met Patrick J. Kelly, who had recently arrived in the United States and was employed at Simpson & Crawford.

In 1892, Hens bought out Sheehan's interests in J.F. Sheehan & Company and contacted Kelly, and they embarked on their own, opening a store on May 1 at 488 Main Street, the corner of Mohawk Street (across from Sheehan's). It was a sixty- by eighteen-foot store, and they stocked "ladies and gents furnishings." "Despite the panic of 1893, the firm prospered. In 1896, the adjoining Benson Art Shop was added as a millinery department."[396] The store policy of the founders was described as "Good merchandise at the lowest prices."[397]

In January 1898, it cleared out the last of J.F. Sheehan & Company's stock at its store, which had grown considerably to include 478, 480, 482, 484, 486 and 488 Main Street.[398] Hens & Kelly was an early adopter of S&H Green Stamps, a rewards program that provided stamps with each purchase, which in turn could be used to purchase items from a catalogue.

In 1905, the partners filed a business certificate as Hens, Kelly & Company, the following year incorporating as the Hens-Kelly Company, with Albert C. Henderson as secretary and treasurer and $600,000 capital. They refiled in 1909 as Hens & Kelly Company and Hens & Kelly Inc. Henderson was no longer involved, but Arthur P. Wesp and William T. Damon were now part of the organization.

"In 1907, despite another depression, the building at the rear was added."[399] As business grew, so did their building needs. "In 1908 the several buildings were made into one."[400] The store continued to flourish

The Hens & Kelly Department Store grew quickly in its early years. This is a newspaper ad from 1897. *Author's collection.*

until 1922, when it embarked on a $1 million ($13 million) expansion plan. Its plan involved no lost sales days, as it built on the site of the current store. The construction began on the Pearl Street side, with the business moving to the Main Street side. The six-story addition (with accommodations for ten stories) had "Jewettville face brick, with limestone trimming, will be fireproof throughout and will embody the latest developments in ventilating, heating and plumbing."[401]

To accommodate men who generally hated to shop, "a special entrance for men will be provided on Mohawk Street, opening directly into the men's department."[402] Buffalo-based Bley & Lyman was the architectural firm. The new $10,000 addition was opened in November 1925, in time to celebrate the thirty-third anniversary of the company.

Business volume doubled every four years from its inception until at least 1925. The two partners never retired, with Kelly saying, "I would rather wear out than rust out."[403] He died in 1927.

This is the Hens & Kelly flagship store at 478 Main Street, circa 1965, when traffic still ruled Main Street. The building is in use today as offices. *Courtesy of Buffalo State College Archives,* Courier-Express *Collection.*

In April 1928, thieves bound two night watchmen in the store at about 7:00 a.m. After breaking the lock to the safe, they used nitroglycerin to blow up the inner door and were able to escape with $20,000 ($255,000).[404]

In May 1935, Arthur P. Wesp was elected president of the firm, succeeding Hens, who had died the month before. In December 1950, it opened its first branch store, at 2262 Seneca Street in South Buffalo, which had been abandoned by Jahraus-Braun when it abruptly closed its doors. The store was open until 1959. P.M. Berst furniture store took over the building in 1961.

Hens & Kelly opened another branch in the L.B. Smith Plaza on Abbott Road in Lackawanna six months later and later opened stores at 2863 Bailey Avenue and in the Transitown Plaza in Clarence.[405] In 1960, it opened "the largest suburban department store in the Buffalo metro area,"[406] at the South Shore Plaza in Hamburg, New York. The $4 million ($29.4 million) store included "the largest S&H Green Stamps redemption center in western New York."[407] Developer Roxie Gian owned both the Transitown and South Shore Plazas.

"The next phase of the Hens & Kelly expansion program will be even more exciting," it was said. At a ceremony held on October 30, 1959, gold-plated time capsules were placed in the brick wall of Hens & Kelly–South Shore. These capsules contain the signatures and messages of the Hens & Kelly Board of Directors, officers and forty-five members of its management group. In addition, all of its associates had their signatures and messages on a sixty-foot-long scroll that was encased in a king-sized time capsule and preserved for posterity in the building.[408]

The company continued its

Hens & Kelly was such a big supporter of S&H Green Stamps that Sperry & Hutchinson later purchased the chain. *Author's collection.*

expansion in an attempt to dominate the local landscape. In 1961, it opened a store in the Northtown Plaza in Amherst, stating, "We have completed the first phase of our expansion into all the major suburban areas of Buffalo."

Sperry & Hutchinson Company, better known for its S&H Green Stamps system, purchased Hens & Kelly in 1967, figuring that it was cheaper to own the retailer than sell to it. Hens & Kelly's expansion continued as it opened stores in the Como Mall, Aurora Village Shopping Center and Summit Park Mall.

By the mid-1970s, things weren't as rosy for Hens & Kelly, or Sperry, as sales were not up to expectations, and Sperry was ready to sell off some assets. Almy Stores Inc. of Boston was interested in Hens & Kelly, but talks broke down in January 1978. Twin Fair Inc., the Buffalo-based discount retailer, purchased the chain in March 1978. In June 1978, Hens & Kelly, in turn, purchased local clothing retailer Peller & Mure.[409]

Twin Fair hoped to revive the chain, saying that it was a great addition to its portfolio, and operated it as an autonomous division. The timing was wrong, though, as Hens & Kelly was on the downward slide, and its sluggish sales began to bring the entire company down.

The first store Hens & Kelly closed was the flagship Main Street store in August 1981. Twin Fair posted its first financial loss in 1980 and attributed it to the Hens & Kelly purchase. It then closed the Como Mall location. By November 1981, things were looking grim for the eighty-nine-year-old company. Three more stores were closed, and the company had a "35 percent off sale," which only pushed the chain into the ranks of a discount merchandiser—not surprising, considering who its owner was. The rest of the stores "followed like dominoes, and by February 12, 1982, the last Hens & Kelly store was locked for good."[410]

In its 1981 annual report, Twin Fair Inc. noted that "Hens & Kelly sales had declined principally due to the depressed economy in western New York."[411] The trend wasn't just restricted to Buffalo but rather was noticeable across the country, and 1982 was the year of the death knell for many retailers. By December 1982, five creditors of the former store chain, including suppliers and plaza owners, tried to force the closed store into voluntary bankruptcy.[412]

The saga of Twin Fair continued, as detailed elsewhere in this book, but the remains of Hens & Kelly still dot our landscape, and several of the freestanding stores have been reused. The early 1980s were not kind to Western New York and its retailers, with unemployment high and stores like Hens & Kelly unable to compete with deep-pocketed national retailers.

In 2006, you could still see signs of Hens & Kelly at its South Shore Plaza location. The interior was unused but deteriorated, and the exterior still had a portion of the original sign. As of early 2007, family members and concerned citizens attempted to have the scrolls saved from the walls of the South Shore Plaza store, which was scheduled for demolition to make way for a new Walmart store. In November 2007, fifty-four small scrolls were found while workers tore down the walls.[413] A small piece of history recovered in the rubble.

Year founded: 1880
Year closed: 1982

Jahraus-Braun Company

When brothers-in-law Fred C. Jahraus and William G. Braun formed their store in 1914, they had no idea how popular it would become. The first store was located at 977–979 Broadway, at the corner of Gibson Street. "The firm has operated one of the foremost department stores of the Broadway-Fillmore district."[414]

The store continued to grow and opened a branch at 2262–2266 Seneca Street in South Buffalo in about 1928. At the same time, a shoe branch was opened at 3041 Bailey Avenue. In 1939, the company took over the former Erion's Department Store at 1021–1027 Broadway. It added new departments such as candy and continued the Erion shoe department in the thrift basement. Local architectural firm Bley & Lyman did the redesign work on the building.

The company continued to operate through World War II, right up until Fred Jahraus died in 1950, which started the firm on a downward tumble. The company filed for bankruptcy in July 1950 and closed the Seneca Street store, leasing it to another local chain, Hens & Kelly. In September of that year, a legal battle broke out between the bankrupt firm and the building owner of the Seneca Street store over the lease of that property.

As the company attempted to stave off creditors, it held a "reorganization sale," but eventually everything failed and the company closed the doors of its Broadway store in 1951. William Braun died in 1957, having watched his dream die a slow death.

Year founded: 1914
Year closed: 1951

The Knowles & Gardner Company

This story will surprise many who have never heard of this millinery and dry goods firm.

The Knowles & Gardner Company was started by Hugh Alexander Knowles and R. Jefferson Gardner as a dry goods store. They opened for business about 1893 at 563–565 Main Street, which ran through to 546–550 Washington Street. The store occupied three floors, including a floor of Japanese novelties. Mrs. Knowles was a successful businesswoman in her own right and supervised the millinery department.

In 1898, the company devoted an entire floor to its bicycle department, "where a riding school will be conducted, and all purchasers will here be taught to ride free of charge."[415]

"In business circles, Knowles was a notoriously poor business man."[416] He purchased a cheap stock of goods in about 1900 on credit, and when the creditors realized that the company was insolvent, they forced it to incorporate and gave Knowles and Gardner each one share of stock. This forced an August 1900 bankruptcy sale.

The store, known as the Knowles & Gardner Drygoods Company, continued with Knowles as president. Unfortunately for the creditors, this did not stop the bleeding. The lack of business ability by Knowles was blamed for the business failing a second time.

"The H.B. Claflin Company of New York was the biggest creditor, and the largest stockholder when the firm incorporated."[417] Creditors thought that fraud may have been involved, and apparently Knowles tried to say that he had invested a larger share than he did, but the lawyers saw through it.

Mrs. Knowles died in May 1902, and Mr. Knowles took over her successful millinery business. The following month, a going-out-of-business sale was held for Knowles & Gardner, "the beginning of the end." Everything was sold to pay off the creditors. By November 1902, Mrs. Knowles's estate was burdened with debts, and Mr. Knowles asked to be removed as administrator of her estate. He appointed attorney Henry L. Schwartz in his place.

A fire started on January 7, 1903, at the former Main Street store, causing $200,000 in damage to the building, contents of the former store and other stores. Knowles's home on Prospect Avenue was foreclosed around mid-1903. The loss of the business, the mismanagement of his late wife's affairs and the foreclosure apparently sat heavy on Knowles's head. On February 26, 1904, Knowles visited attorney Schwartz in his private office in the Marine Bank building. There he shot Schwartz three times and killed him. He wanted attorney Baker also and threatened to shoot any police officer who got in his way. After holding the police at bay for a short time, he turned the gun on himself and put a bullet through his temple, instantly ending his life.

Schwartz was a member of the law firm that employed the attorneys for the receiver, Leo Frank, of the defunct Knowles & Gardener.[418]

Year founded: 1893
Year closed: 1902

S.O. BARNUM & SON

One of Buffalo's most unique stores was S.O. Barnum & Son Company, better known as Barnum's. Stephen Ostrom Barnum was born in Utica, New York, in 1816 and partnered with his father in a store known as Barnum's Bazar in 1838. It was said to be "the largest house of its kind between New York City and Chicago."[419]

He set out for Buffalo in 1845 and opened a variety store at 211 Main Street, the heart of the business district at the time, with his brother Richard S. The six-story store had "nearly 53,000 square feet" of floor space.[420] Richard only stayed a short time, probably until the business was actually running sufficiently, and then moved to Chicago to open a similar store with another brother.[421]

The early store carried "Yankee notions," which best describes the "mammoth stock of merchandise."[422] It carried a wide range of items, including toys, and "Santa Claus has made his headquarters there ever since S.O. Barnum arrived in Buffalo."[423]

Barnum "stamped his own individuality on his variety store and that individuality has not been lost during growth and change of management."[424] Barnum was "several times associated in partnership. William Woltge was bought out in 1872 and the partnership between himself, Julius P. Wahl, John Ansteth and John S. Smith was dissolved in 1880."[425]

In 1870, the company was called S.O. Barnum's Sons & Company, eventually becoming S.O. Barnum & Son Company when his son, Theodore Downs Barnum, joined the firm. Apparently, a long court case between Stephen Barnum and former partner Julius Wahl took nineteen years and several of Buffalo's top lawyers, including John G. Milburn and Adelbert Moot, to conclude.[426]

The company developed a slogan to go along with its huge variety: "Go to Barnum's First!" It was always the last resort if you couldn't find it anywhere else.[427] One reason why it had everything was because it never got rid of anything. Unlike other stores that wanted to turn over their inventory, "Barnum's simply tucked it away, expecting that some day there might be a call for it."[428]

Stephen Barnum died in early October 1899. On October 4, 1938, the company announced that it would be liquidating its merchandise and going out of business.[429] For the first time in the company's history, cash registers would be in the store, which had always used "an old-fashioned overhead cash conveyor system"[430] that was considered ancient even in 1938. It would be the company liquidating the store that would be using them, though. The only reason that could be found for the store closing was the aftereffects of the Depression, which hurt most all kinds of businesses.

The people of Buffalo lamented the loss when the store held its first and only sale and closed its doors forever. The building, which was renumbered 265 Main Street in the 1800s, held several businesses over the years. The last was Millington Lockwood Inc. in 1963 before a $250,000 ($1.78 million) five-alarm fire destroyed the building.[431]

Barnum's cast-iron store sign was donated to the Buffalo Historical Society (now the Buffalo History Museum) for use in its 1870 street display.[432]

Year founded: 1845
Year closed: 1938

Sattler's

At one time, there was an abundant number of Buffalo retailing institutions, and like many of them, Sattler's started in a small storefront with an idea and a dream.

John G. Sattler was but seventeen years old when he decided to turn the front room of his mother's home at 992 Broadway into a shoe store. "The Broadway Market Shoe House" was painted on the front window, and he opened shop in 1889. The store, located near Fillmore Avenue, was stocked with men's and ladies' shoes and was a hit almost from day one. By 1922, it was the largest retail shoe store between New York City and Chicago,[433] doing $400,000 ($5.2 million) per year in sales.

Sattler bought properties adjacent to his as the store grew until 1900, when a "larger, more modern building" was constructed.[434] The store's main address at this time was changed to 998 Broadway.

In 1926, his twenty-two-year-old son-in-law, Charles Hahn Jr., joined him as part owner and began the transformation that would forever change Buffalo retailing. They began by adding a work clothes department. "Mr. Sattler would stand at the front door of the store to welcome customers and bid them goodbye."[435] "I used to ask every person who left the store without a package why he didn't buy anything. That's how I found out what my customers wanted that we didn't have in stock," Sattler was quoted as saying.[436]

In 1927, Hahn hired Aaron Rabow, also in his twenties, as a buyer of women's wear[437] for a small dress department that Sattler had added.[438]

This Sattler's celebration featured (left to right) founder John Sattler (standing), Aaron Rabow and Charles Hahn. *Courtesy of the Voorhees family.*

He would eventually run the company. The two young men "saw no reason why shoe customers couldn't be sold everything else they needed as well."[439]

Then, to accomplish their goal, they hired nineteen-year-old newspaperman Robert S. Cornelius as advertising and promotion manager of Sattler's. They gradually added departments, and the three created "Hellzapoppin'-styled promotions." These sometimes wild and wacky promotions changed Buffalo advertising, "and soon Sattler's was known far and wide in retailing circles."[440] The store had "outlandish promotional schemes. Cars would be given away each week. High wire walkers would thrill shoppers out in the street." They would load the front windows with canned goods that customers purchased by the case.

During the heyday of the 1940s, the store would advertise some big purchase, such as the stock of a bankrupt store, or a fire sale or one of many promotions. It bought name-brand products at extreme discounts and passed them along to its customers. It would have movie and radio stars at

One of the interesting marketing promotions that Sattler's did brought the widow of infamous train engineer Casey Jones to town. *Left to right:* Aaron Rabow, Mrs. Casey Jones and Charles Hahn. *Courtesy of the Voorhees family.*

the store on Mondays coinciding with big sales—anything that would bring in the throngs of customers it needed on a daily basis.

Bob Cornelius spoke before a group that was discussing the technique of brainstorming, probably in the mid-1950s:

> *We have been using brainstorming at Sattler's for about twenty-one years. For many, many years we used it more or less secretly, in the Advertising and Sales Promotion Division—secretly because we didn't want any brass in.*
>
> *Sattler's is somewhat different from most stores in that we live on store traffic. We live on store traffic day by day. The telephone means nothing. They have to come into the store.*
>
> *Now, we do a lot of things that a number of stores might consider beneath their dignity. We do it to bring people into the store. After we get them in there and expose our merchandise to them, they buy. But if we don't bring them into the store, we don't do business. So we have to continually dream up ideas to get hordes of people into the store.*

We clock over a hundred thousand people in the store on many single days. When we quit clocking big crowds like that, we are going to quit being Sattler's. We are located two miles from the downtown section. We have no theaters—we have one sort of scratch-angle, old branch theater out there—but we have no theaters, no restaurants, no hotels—none of the things that normally bring crowds to downtown areas. We have to depend on our own crowd bringing ideas.

Now, Sattler's has throughout the years brainstormed such things and come up with such idea's as our Bargain Train, where we dramatize the idea that, "Sattler's buys by carloads so you can buy for less."

"Fast Freight to 998." That is our well-known store address in Buffalo. We say, "From the Eastern Shore to the Wonder Store, from the Golden Gate to 998, the Bargain Train is rattling across the country to bring you the best buys, best because Sattler's buys in carload lots."

We got out of the brainstorming session the idea of bringing Mrs. Casey Jones, the widow of old Casey Jones, to Buffalo from Jackson, Tennessee, where the old lady now lives.

Mrs. Casey Jones came to Sattler's as a guest, her fare to Buffalo taken care of by the railroad. She was handed over the bridal suite in the Hotel Statler. She appeared on nine separate radio and television shows, each time mentioning the fact that she was here to open Sattler's Bargain Train promotion for that particular year.

One time when Sattler's had just been the subject of an article in <u>Coronet</u> magazine, that told about some of our screwball brainstormed ideas, a lady from New River, Massachusetts, wrote and said, "I read all about you in <u>Coronet</u> magazine, but I never expect to get to Buffalo. I read about your wonderful bargains. Here is fifty cents. See what you can send me for this."

We sent an American Airlines Flagship down to Albany, as close as we could get, brought her over to Albany in a cavalcade of automobiles supplied by dealers of that area, brought her back to Buffalo, and ensconced her in the bridal suite of the Hotel Statler. The next morning she was our guest at the store, where employees came down before the store opened and conducted a parade welcoming Mrs. Johnson, and we advertised to the public that we were going to have Mrs. Johnson as our guest and show how hospitable we could be to a customer who had sent fifty cents for a bargain.

Finally, as she stepped onto the American Airlines airplane to go back to Albany, we handed back to her eleven cents and said, "That only cost you thirty-nine cents at Sattler's. You get a real bargain here."

We also have brainstormed such ideas as our Bargain Airlift…that took place at the same time that the Berlin Airlift was at its most dramatic height.

We went to the Pentagon with this brainstormed thing that people told us was ridiculous and came back with an all day show, with three jet teams, two of them from American Aviation groups, one from the Navy, and one from the Air Force.

The Canadian Government heard about our air show, and said, "Can we put in a jet team?" I told them yes, if you will send down thirteen bombers to escort them and they did.

We had an air show that lasted from nine o'clock in the morning until six o'clock at night. Everybody in Buffalo had a sunburned face that day, May 8, 1949, when we had over $60,000,000 [$549 million] worth of aviation equipment flying for a Buffalo department store.

Our brainstormed airlift wound up with such things as every airline in the entire area rerouting its planes to fly over Sattler's. We had floodlights going up into the sky. Three airlines banded together and flew a seven-million-year-old cake of glacier ice from Juneau, Alaska, to cool the cocktails at the press luncheon. That's no lie.

We flew lobsters from Maine, strawberries from Florida, tomatoes from Louisiana; we had our buyers up all hours of the night, meeting airplanes at the airport, to take off lots of merchandise and get their pictures taken.

The thing wound up as the National Retail Dry Goods Association's winner of that year for the best coordinated campaign.[441]

The store had more than fifty-two thousand square feet of space when Hahn added four thousand more, and by 1931, it had another thirty thousand square feet. Rabow, with increased responsibilities, added more departments, including men's, boys', furniture, appliances, housewares and a food market.[442]

In 1932, the store was incorporated as Sattler's Inc. with Sattler, Hahn and Sattler's daughters, Marion and Doris, as sole shareholders. Business continued to prosper. In late 1939, they purchased thirty houses along Gibson and Beck Streets, which sided the store, to add a two-acre parking lot to accommodate five hundred cars.[443] Aaron Rabow had become general manager by this time.

The company didn't forget its employees either during many of the expansions. In 1939, the eight hundred employees had a "beach club" on the store roof, with miniature golf, horseshoe courts and shuffleboard.[444]

Plans for a fifth expansion were unveiled in late March 1940 that added three floors and more facilities for its employees, plus about two acres of floor

Sattler's Bargain Train was a great promotion that brought customers into the store by the thousands. *Courtesy of the Voorhees family.*

space to the rear of the building, "increasing the store's facilities by 50 per cent."[445] A new rear entrance from the massive parking lot was also added.

After the end of World War II, Sattler's continued its expansion. In December 1945, it completed the purchase of "most of the properties in Broadway between the present Sattler's Department Store and Beck Street." The $175,000 ($2.12 million) expansion added a four-story U-shaped building surrounding A.S. Beck and Winch's.[446]

The expansion and building frenzy under Hahn's leadership (John Sattler had died in 1941) continued in late 1946, when "the cornerstone for a $2 million addition…was laid" on the fifty-seventh anniversary of the store's founding.[447] It added 106,000 square feet, and the store now had 365,000 square feet of selling space at 998 Broadway. It also planned to increase employment by 50 percent and "install the largest food market of its kind in the United States" with the expansion.[448] When the huge undertaking debuted in September 1947, the store added home heating, insulation, power tools, sewing machine, roofing, siding and more departments.[449]

The grand opening included the "playing of 800 specially recorded jingles over radio stations, rotogravure advertisements," among other promotions.[450] The final cost of the expansion was $2.75 million ($26.8 million).[451]

That fall, Sattler's had its first Santa Claus parade down Broadway. It would become a tradition that would last for many years.

In June 1950, a turbulent zoning board meeting at Buffalo City Hall pitted Sattler's against the East Side community it occupied. Sattler's requested a permit to expand its receiving facilities and parking lot, but the nearby residents resented the traffic congestion caused by the stores on Broadway.[452]

Attorney Howard T. Saperston, representing Sattler's, told the board and angry crowd that it was in everyone's best interests to approve the request since it would provide an additional two hundred parking spaces. The company feared that without the additional spaces it would start losing customers to suburban stores, where ample parking was already available.[453] According to one resident, the traffic congestion on Beck and Gibson Streets was "particularly acute when the stores are open Monday, Thursday and Saturday evenings."[454]

In February 1953, rumors started to spread that Hahn, who owned 80 percent of Sattler's stock, was interested in selling the business.[455] The rumors originated in New York City, where Herbert J. Vogelsang, president of First National Bank of Buffalo, first heard them while meeting with a friend. With an interest to keep the store locally owned, and possibly pick up a new client, Vogelsang worked quietly behind the scenes. He helped to arrange financing through several insurance companies and convinced one of his customers, Irving I. Levick, owner of Seneca Warehouse & Industrial Center Inc. at 701 Seneca Street, to finance the $500,000 down payment.

When Hahn agreed to the deal, he knew that Levick was one of the buyers but was unaware of who his backers were and didn't know until he signed the papers.[456] That could have been a devastating mistake to the community since he apparently had not specifically looked for a local buyer.

The $7 million ($57.1 million) transaction by Associated Investors Inc., of which Levick was the main shareholder, was completed on June 29, 1953. Vogelsang gained Sattler's as a new banking client, and Aaron Rabow became president of Sattler's, which was grossing about $27 million ($220 million) in sales.[457]

As Sattler's continued under its new owners, expansion outside its East Side location was now on its mind. In February 1954, the company leased the former Jahraus-Braun store at 1021 Broadway from the new owners. It turned that store into Sattler's Home Annex store, where it sold appliances, and then added an appliance store at 3610 Main Street and in the University Plaza. The year 1957 proved to be a busy one as the

A parade in front of Sattler's welcoming home Buffalo Bob Smith of *Howdy Doody* fame. Clarabell the Clown can be seen sitting in the second car. *Courtesy of the Voorhees family.*

company purchased Household Outfitting Company Inc. of Buffalo[458] and renamed it Sattler's. It opened another appliance store in Hamburg in June 1957.

Sattler's growth continued with the opening of a branch in the Thruway Plaza in 1957 featuring youth apparel, as well as a trade-in store at 1025 Broadway. It also purchased the Ernst Kern Company, Detroit, Michigan's third-largest and third-generation department store.[459] "Following numerous corporate problems and changes in management, the [Kern] store closed its doors for the final time on December 23, 1959."[460] Apparently, it wasn't sure what to do with the store.

John T. Madden, a Sattler's vice-president and treasurer, resigned in September 1959 in order to open an insurance agency inside of Sattler's. His son was in the insurance industry and joined him in the operation. The move allowed Ralph H. Wilcove the opportunity to take his position, and Paul Shulman was promoted to vice-president and controller.[461]

In 1961, it began consolidating its appliance stores by closing the University, Main Street and Hamburg stores and moving everything to the Annex store. In 1962, a $3 million ($21.6 million) 200,000-square-foot store at the new Boulevard Mall in Amherst was built.[462] The new mall featured many names now gone: Kleinhans, Jenss, Bond Clothes, S.S. Kresge, F.W. Woolworth, Acme Supermarkets, Gray Drug Company, A.S. Beck, Thom McAn and Flagg Shoes.[463]

By Easter 1962, the company was planning to open two stores in suburban Rochester, New York.[464] One was opened in 1962, and the other was never built. The expansion, remodeling at 998 Broadway and the home store and the new Boulevard Mall store overextended the firm. In June 1963, it announced the closing of the Rochester store because it took "so much manpower and our time that it has become physically impossible to conduct our Rochester store as it should be."[465]

In 1963, Sattler's Drugs Inc. opened four free-standing stores plus added a pharmacy inside each Sattler's store. When the company celebrated its seventy-fifth anniversary in 1964, it did it in grand style. There was a motorcade from city hall to 998 Broadway and a ribbon-cutting ceremony with company officials and Polish American mayor Chester Kowal, while the Thruway Plaza and Boulevard Mall stores also celebrated with ribbon-cutting ceremonies. At 9:00 p.m., the Boulevard Mall store had a huge fireworks display.

That year, Sattler's joined together with Loblaws and Star Discount Food Stores (owned by Loblaws) to offer a certificate program where the customer could buy a certificate good for 25 percent off at Sattler's.[466]

As it continued its expansion, it opened a $5 million ($35.6 million) 500,000-square-foot warehouse and home furnishings and food store, all under one roof. The facility was a former plant that Sattler's expanded at 1803 Elmwood and Hertel Avenues in North Buffalo.[467] Sattler's Wonderful World of Foods Inc. and Home Furnishings City U.S.A. opened in September 1965. It was called "a giant step forward in space age selling, bold and imaginative merchandising."[468]

The company's sales growth had increased 50 percent over the previous two years, and it expected similar future growth.[469] The next year, Sattler's owner Irving Levick purchased the former Kobacker's store at 1018 Broadway.[470]

New rumors about the sale of Sattler's began to circulate in early August 1968. It was doing about $50 million ($313 million) in sales[471] when Coburn Corporation of America was set to buy the company. Coburn was not in the retail business, and the transaction would have made Irving Levick one of its largest shareholders.[472] The sale never went through, but the Koffman family of Binghamton, New York (owners of a loan company), stepped in and made a private purchase in 1969.

Sattler's continued its expansion into the suburbs by opening a store in 1969 in the new Seneca Mall in West Seneca. Again abandoning what made it successful, the new store was similar to the Boulevard Mall store, which was an upscale department store, with completely different product mixes than what Sattler's customer's had come to expect.[473]

"The Sattler's shift from the old bargain basement atmosphere comes across in the high fashion, women's wear section." They sold art reproductions and had a pet shop, sporting goods and an appliance department. Although company president Ralph Wilcove claimed that it wanted to "maintain price leadership,"[474] this store would eventually be one of the catalysts that brought the business to its knees.

New rumors that the company was for sale were in the air in January 1970 and were confirmed by the E.J. Korvette Company (a chain of discount department stores), which was interested in purchasing the company. Sattler's denied the rumor. In July 1972, it closed the Thruway Plaza store, citing its small size[475] and probably its proximity to the newer Seneca Mall store.

When Kobacker's closed in the Main Place Mall in early 1973, Sattler's seized the opportunity to open a store downtown. At about the same time, it remodeled its flagship store at 998 Broadway and moved the home furnishing store into 998 from across the street at 1021 Broadway.[476]

When Buffalo-based financial services company Firstmark Corporation decided to expand into the retail field in 1976, it purchased the Sattler's chain.[477] Firstmark was having financial trouble of its own at the time, so the Koffmans traded 500,000 shares of Firstmark stock for Sattler's. The transaction was completed in October.[478]

Sattler's was no longer just a thriving retail chain but rather a pawn to be traded between companies like Monopoly houses. Although each purchaser had kept the main management core together, each successive owner took another bite and another piece of the company was lost. It started when Charles Hahn Jr. made his sale back in 1953, not really knowing who was buying his company. It wouldn't stop until every bit of life was sucked out of the chain, every last light was out and every last brick at 998 Broadway was torn apart.

Sattler's announced that it was returning to Cheektowaga and into the converted Thruway Plaza, which was now the Thruway Mall.[479] It opened a "specialized fashion store" in the former Neisner Brothers store in October 1979. It also opened two stores in the extreme southern tier of Western

Another promo shot for the Sattler's crew, with Aaron Rabow and Charles Hahn. *Courtesy of the Voorhees family.*

New York, at the Olean and Chautauqua Malls. One of the stores was Sattler's Plus, which carried women's plus-sized apparel.[480] Sattler's was now a multidimensional retail chain.

Firstmark announced that Sattler's had lost $117,000 ($391,000) in 1978, attributed to "inflationary factors…an increase in the federal minimum wage, and higher interest costs."[481] Did it think that Sattler's shoppers didn't see that the merchandise mix was no longer the same Sattler's they had grown up with, that the name was diluted by opening upscale department stores and women's clothing stores?

Not wasting any more time than it had to, Firstmark sold Sattler's to Plapinger Enterprises Inc. of Taunton, New Jersey, in August 1979. At least Plapinger had retail experience running the S.P. Dunham & Company chain. "We are enthusiastic about Sattler's and plan to embark on a program of modernizing and updating the entire chain."[482] The sale resulted in a financial loss to Firstmark, which stated that it was going to concentrate on its financial services after the sale. It should have never left. In Firstmark's defense, it later said that Sattler's 998 store was losing close to $10,000 per week while it owned the company.[483]

By this time, the East Side neighborhood around the Sattler's flagship store had declined. The demographics had changed, and many of its customers had moved to the suburbs and shopped at the suburban stores. On September 1, 1979, Sattler's announced that it planned on closing or selling its drugstore chain and the home furnishings store,[484] as Plapinger was only interested in purchasing the department stores. Things moved very quickly, and by the eighteenth, the drugstores were sold to James Confectionery Sales Inc., headed by former Sattler's Drugs vice-president Gerald Bornstein. It just closed the home furnishings store.

When Plapinger (later named United Department Stores Inc.) took over on October 1, 1979, Ralph Wilcove resigned as president. Plapinger, in turn, brought in fourteen new top executives, including Gerald P. Nathason, a partner in Plapinger, as president. "I have one goal here and that is that Sattler's will be the best department store in Buffalo, bar none."[485]

The 998 store was starting to show its age and was downsized since, according to Plapinger, it "has not been profitable." It intended to win customers back through cultural sponsorships and program advertising,[486] not through great deals or Hellzapoppin' sales.

Almost immediately, rumors that it would close 998 began circulating. "If anything happened to Sattler's…you would find the rest of the community collapsed in a business sense," noted a local paper.[487] Banker Wallace S. Piotrowski added, "I psychologically identify Sattler's and the Broadway Market as the center of the Polish East Side."[488]

Although Plapinger said that it wanted to keep the old store open, it was not a mall store, and it depended on traffic coming to it, as illustrated by the passage from Bob Cornelius noted earlier. By late January 1980, it was prepared to spend several million dollars on renovations and to turn the big store into a mini mall.[489] In turn, it asked the city for financial help, or it would have to close the landmark store. The city offered a $2 million interest-free loan, which had to be repaid if it closed.[490]

In late September 1980, United Department Stores purchased a ninety-two-store chain and considered moving its headquarters to Buffalo, which was right in the middle of its holdings.[491] This never materialized, and the purchase would be the bane of United.

The whole deal to remodel Sattler's fell through in late November, and 998 was reduced to a one-floor operation.[492] That changed again in late January 1981 as the store was renamed Sattler's Clearance Center.[493] The Broadway-Fillmore neighborhood needed Sattler's as much as Sattler's needed it, but neither was capable of supporting the other. That same day, one of Buffalo's other retail institutions, Hengerer's, announced that it was merging with Sibley, Lindsay & Curr of Rochester.[494] The face of Buffalo-based retailing was taking a turn for the worse.

The end everyone feared finally came on March 31, 1981, when a "going out of business" permit was purchased at city hall.[495] Some residents felt that the Broadway-Fillmore neighborhood had already hit rock bottom and that the closing of Sattler's was a sign of good things to come. Others knew better. Unfortunately, "the neighborhood is unsure of what it wants."[496] The downward spiral of the whole chain began soon after with the announcement that the Seneca Mall store was unprofitable and would also close.[497] The announcement must have prompted customers to visit the store for some Sattler's bargains since it restocked the store in late November 1981.[498]

It may have been a legal remedy to appease the mall owners because in late January 1982, United Department Stores filed Chapter 11 bankruptcy protection and announced that the Thruway, Seneca and Main Place Mall stores would all close.[499] United said that it thought Sattler's could recover from bankruptcy.[500]

Leaving just the Boulevard Mall store open, Sattler's was a shell of what it had once been. It was now just a name; it wasn't the same and never would be. United and previous owners had felt that changing the company to cater to a different, upscale market was the answer. It obviously wasn't.

Originally, Sattler's "conveyed the concept to their customers that they could get a bargain, not on cheap bargain items, but on high quality merchandise," stated retired controller Paul Shulman. Its crazy promotions and antics are what made it money hand over fist and, at the same time, made it unlike any other Buffalo store.[501]

The end finally arrived in December 1982 when United Department Stores announced the closing of the last Sattler's store, located in the Boulevard Mall.[502] When it exactly closed is not really important anymore. Sattler's began dying with each successive purchaser and was nearly dead when United Department Stores purchased the chain in 1979. United hurried the process by adding its own financial woes to the mix. When it closed the 998 Broadway store, Sattler's was, in essence, already dead.

The store died an unceremonious death. All the items left in the building—display racks, shelving, office furniture, even a photo seen elsewhere in this book—were up for a final bargain sale. The liquidator was letting cartloads go for a buck. Maybe Bob Cornelius and the rest of the promotions people would have been proud of the deals, but not at the expense of the hard work they had put in many years before.

The building that was built, expanded and became a great Buffalo institution and a symbol of Buffalo's Polish East Side was demolished in 1989. A Kmart store was later constructed on the site, kept open for a short time and then subsequently also closed.

To this day, if you ask a Buffalonian of a certain age if they remember 998, they immediately know what you are talking about and start to reminisce. "Shop and save at Sattler's, Nine-nine-eight Broadway in Buff-a-lowwwww…" would never be heard again.

Year founded: 1889
Year closed: 1982

WILLIAM HENGERER COMPANY (HENGERER'S)

One of Buffalo's oldest retail establishments started way back in 1836 when Richard J. Sherman opened a dry goods store at 155 Main on Swan Street in Buffalo. By 1869, he had partnered with J.C. Barnes to form Sherman & Barnes & Company. William Hengerer came to the United States from Germany when he was ten years old, and when he was twenty-two, he moved to Buffalo from Pittsburgh, joining Sherman & Barnes as a clerk.[503] He enlisted in the army and served two years during the Civil War,[504] afterward returning to his clerk position.

The firm later split. Barnes formed J.C. Barnes & Company in early 1867, followed by Barnes & Bancroft (with James K. Bancroft) in 1869 at 259 Main Street. Hengerer was admitted as a partner in 1873, the firm becoming Barnes, Bancroft & Company. "How thoroughly he [Hengerer] deserved it is best shown by results since then."[505]

In 1885, the firm became Barnes, Hengerer & Company—the principals being Barnes, who now resided in New York City; Hengerer; John C. Nagel; Bancroft; and Clarence O. Howard. Barnes supplied $300,000 ($7.1 million) in initial capital and Bancroft $100,000 ($2.34 million).

Late on February 1, 1888, a great fire of suspicious circumstance blazed away in the store, eventually engulfing twelve other connected businesses on the "Iron Block." Although the fire was devastating, collapsing the entire building in thirty minutes, the business would carry on. "Almost before the fire was out buyers were sent to New York post haste for new goods, and inside of two weeks they were ready for business again in a very much smaller store."[506]

Five months later, a fourteen-year-old former clerk at the store confessed to starting the $1.25 million ($29.6 million) fire and subsequently attempting to start the ruins up several times, all out of spite for an unknown incident. After the fire, a new store was built on the same site, and the transformation from a dry goods store to a department store began. It added a furniture department, an employee lunchroom, delivery wagons and what the company called "a fresh grip on trade."[507]

The firm continued in its present state until 1892, when Bancroft exited the partnership; Barnes died in 1895. At that time, the William Hengerer Company was formed. "From the moment Mr. Hengerer assumed the reins the policy of the store has been more and more aggressive until the pendulum has swung from ultra-conservatism to 'first in everything.'"[508] The store was "the first [in Buffalo] to inaugurate Saturday half-holidays during the summer months, the first to close for Decoration Day [Memorial Day] and the first to observe Labor Day as a general holiday."[509]

Hengerer insisted on fixing prices by cost, not value, and also insisted on "the truth in all advertisements."[510] By 1897, it had more than six hundred employees, $1 million in merchandise and was said to be the biggest department store between New York City and Chicago. "In all the 30 years history of the business the standard of quality has never been lowered and the mark of satisfaction never overlooked."[511] The store purchased top-quality goods, never "seconds" or bankruptcy sales. Business prospered under Hengerer's leadership.

With business growing, the company needed larger quarters. In 1903, the Phoenix Hotel, which had replaced the Tifft House, which was home to Grover Cleveland before his rise to the presidency, was demolished to make way for a new store.[512] The company constructed a six-story building at 457–471 Main Street. One of the most striking features was to be an immense glass dome that would surmount the center of the store, above an open-air court that would extend from the basement to the roof.[513]

No one could go through the store of the William Hengerer Company without a certain sense of personal pride, a pride inspired by the knowledge that it was a Buffalo store, built up by Buffalonians, managed by Buffalonians and largely for the benefit of Buffalonians.[514]

The new building meant that the company could offer its customers even more modern conveniences. It added a telegraph office, a post office, public telephones, refrigerated drinking water and "the largest grocery store in Buffalo." It reused marble from the old Tifft House in the employees' "toilet-rooms." Local architects Cyrus K. Porter & Sons designed the building.[515]

This was Main Street in Buffalo, taken in about 1904. Several retail firms can be seen in the photo, but the William Hengerer store is the white building on the right. *Courtesy of Library of Congress, Detroit Publishing Company Photograph Collection.*

On April 30, 1904, it moved into its shiny new store. It all sounded wonderful, but less than a year after moving into the new building, William Hengerer announced that he was selling the company to a good friend of his, and this would forever change the future of the business.

On March 17, 1901, Hengerer said, "The William Hengerer Company has been sold to William H. Hotchkiss, president of J.N. Adam & Company, who becomes absolute owner of the Hengerer business." The reason was understandable, as Mr. Hengerer was ill and planned to move to a warmer climate.[516] He was in Los Angeles but a week when he died in early December 1905.

A little over a month after Hotchkiss purchased Hengerer's, he arranged a business transaction unlike any seen in Buffalo retailing up to that time. On April 12, 1905, the H.B. Claflin & Company of New York City, headed by John Claflin, purchased both J.N. Adam and the William Hengerer Company.[517] For Hotchkiss, Christmas certainly came early that year.

In 1910, with business doing well, the company added three additional stories to the building on Main Street.[518] Edward L. Hengerer, son of the founder, had joined the company in about 1903 as treasurer. He was recognized for his financial skills by parent company Associated Dry Goods (formerly H.B. Claflin) and was sent to New York City in 1915 to join Lord & Taylor as vice-president and general merchandising manager. He returned to Buffalo in 1917 and took over as president of Hengerer's.

The company spent $1 million ($17 million) on renovations to the store in 1927, which included a new granite terra-cotta façade, revolving doors and "invisible glass" display windows.[519]

Hengerer's never missed a chance to celebrate its anniversary and have a sale, often retelling the company's origins in its sale ads. This helped to push its "local" appeal, even though it hadn't been locally owned since 1905.

In late April 1929, company president Edward L. Hengerer announced his resignation. "Of course he didn't resign," noted one of the newspaper editorials. The theory was the New York City owners were "through" with him and wanted one of their own in charge:

> *In the battle between dollars and human lives, hopes and ambitions, dollars win, and never so mercilessly as in this glorious era of "big business."*
>
> *Alien corporations with their "fire" sales and three ball signs line the streets with a liberal sprinkling of "For Rent" signs—graves of local merchants who couldn't stand the gaff—"Bigger better and busier in Buffalo." Their interest in Buffalo is limited to what they can suck out of it.*[520]

The dismantling of Buffalo's locally owned businesses was slowly taking place. After Edward L. Hengerer resigned in mid-June, Prentiss T. Burtis was brought in as his replacement. Burtis resigned in 1935[521] and was replaced by J. Edward Davidson, who had been a vice-president at Macy's in New York City.[522]

In 1936, Hengerer's celebrated its 100th anniversary, and in mid-1937, it began another modernization program, which was unveiled in March 1938 and completed in September at a cost of $1 million ($15.5 million). A large addition, a new façade, new departments, thirty-six thousand square feet of new space and a "glass brick penthouse has been built for office workers."[523]

Like most upscale stores of the time, Hengerer's had a tearoom, Miss Vincent's Tea Room, which was a popular gathering place for the ladies after they had spent the afternoon shopping in the store.

In August 1941, the store began staying open late on Thursdays to allow all the defense workers a chance to shop.[524] After the end of the war (1946), the company expanded again by leasing 475 Main and 460 Washington Streets, purchasing 479–483 Main, 11–13 Mohawk and 462 Washington Streets in what was a $1 million ($11.2 million) transaction. Current company president Harold M. Hecht said that it was the "most important step in store history since its locating on the present site on May 9, 1904."[525]

In September 1946, it purchased the Howard Brothers building at 457–459 Washington and an adjoining parking lot. It would utilize the building for "non-selling purposes."[526] In August 1947, it announced plans for its first branch store, not locally but rather in Batavia, New York, about midway between Buffalo and Rochester, New York. The store opened in October.[527]

In 1951, it expanded again, adding an addition at 465 Main Street and moving Miss Vincent's Tea Room to the adjacent Rand Building, with an entrance from inside Hengerer's.[528] Several floors were expanded, and new shops were added. The cost was $400,000 ($3.36 million).[529]

In what was a common marketing promotion used by department stores of the time, a complete seven-room house was built inside the store. The scale house was built by a local construction company that just happened to be building the same type of house in the Buffalo suburb of Eggerstville.[530]

One of the most interesting jobs in Buffalo's department stores was the Hengerer's elevator girl. All the girls were tall blondes who wore deep-blue suits, pearls and white gloves. They made $1.35 per hour, a dime more than minimum wage. The company bought their clothes and shoes, and they had to wear girdles. The store did their hair and makeup every week in the downtown sixth-floor beauty salon, and they had paid lunches. It was better than being a sales clerk, having to buy your own dark clothing for work. In addition to the basic operation of the elevator car, the role of the "Hengerer's Girl" was as a goodwill ambassador to customers, as well as a reporter of trends and comments back to management. Customers' comments about their shopping experience overheard in the elevator were likely a valuable source of intelligence to management. They also had to keep track of the department heads and vendors who were in the store. They were gossip columnists and the "glamour girls of the store."[531]

In 1957, the company opened its first suburban store at 3900 Main Street in, coincidentally enough, Eggerstville, New York. The free-standing structure was not located in or near any large plaza, but it was probably located amid the homes being built by the previously mentioned contractor. In late 1959, parent company Associated Dry Goods announced that it was closing Hengerer's sister store in Buffalo, the J.N. Adam & Company. It was not in the company's best interest to operate two different stores in the same market, let alone on the same street.[532]

With J.N.'s closing, Associated could afford to spend more time and money on Hengerer's, and in February 1960, it did just that, announcing a $1 million ($7.36 million) interior expansion and modernization, including installation of the city's first "air door."[533]

In December 1962, the company announced the purchase of fifty-four acres of land in the suburb of West Seneca to build a 100,000-square-foot store at the future site of the Seneca Mall.[534] In September 1963, it added another addition to the bursting downtown store by opening a new Junior and Young Junior shop in space in the adjacent Rand Building.[535]

As the suburban migration continued, Hengerer's desire to stay close to its customers drove it to the suburbs. Duane Lyman was chosen to be architect of a new store on Sheridan Drive in Tonawanda. The $1 million fifty-thousand-square-foot store was started in 1964.[536]

The Eastern Hills Mall in Clarence was a new development in 1969, and Hengerer's was one of the first tenants.[537] When the store opened in 1971, "[o] pening day volume...was the

dread
struggling
with boots this winter?

Hengerer's
· AMHERST · BUFFALO

Then slip into

ALASKANS

by

Kickerinos

The over-the-stocking boot that fits like a shoe . . . that's toasty warm and so smart looking too! Alaskans are the perfect answer for all day campus wear for they'll go from class to class from building to building in heavenly comfort. Crepe soled in glove-soft leather with cuddly, warm nylon pile lining and furry convertible collar that can be worn up or down. Black, grey, or taffy in sizes 4½ to 10.

13.98

Mail or phone your order — call MO. 6666
BOOTS, HENGERER'S SECOND FLOOR
Also Hengerer's Amherst

In January 1981, Hengerer's merged with sister company Sibley's of Rochester. For a short time, both names appeared on marketing materials and in advertisements. *Author's collection.*

largest of any store opening in the history of Associated Dry Goods... Hengerer's Eastern Hills store will give shoppers...in the Buffalo area a new visual experience, a departure not only from the other Hengerer's stores, but all other retail stores in the community."[538]

Hengerer's had a record year in 1973, with double-digit growth. Only three of the other twenty Associated Dry Goods Corporation chains were specifically mentioned in its annual report, including Sibley, Lindsay & Curr of the neighboring city of Rochester.[539]

Buffalo Savings Bank began its first in-store branches in all the Hengerer's stores in 1976.[540]

Associated Dry Goods began a downward slide in 1974 that would affect every store in its portfolio. By 1978, it was losing money quarterly, which it blamed on fast expansion, too much inventory, high management turnover[541] and an antiquated financial system. As part of the shift to control costs, some of its stores were closed or, in Buffalo's case, merged. Sibley, Lindsay & Curr of Rochester was merged with Hengerer's in January 1981.[542] Sibley's was Rochester's largest retailer, homegrown and beloved. Its flagship store in downtown Rochester took up an entire city block and was purchased by Associated in the late 1950s. Hengerer's, now part of a sixteen-store chain, offered additional product selections that it hadn't carried before.

With the merger of the two stores, one name would have to win out. Maybe it was because Sibley's had stores in Rochester and Syracuse, while Hengerer's was just a Buffalo name, that gave Sibley's an advantage.[543] As a compromise, the company name was changed to Hengerer's & Sibley's, a name that anyone could see wouldn't last.[544]

Just a few days after the announced merger, jobs were eliminated,[545] the Hengerer's warehouse at 255 Great Arrow Drive was closed and operations were moved to Rochester. The fate of the flagship downtown store teetered precariously as decisions were made at the corporate level. The name game didn't last long. On November 9, 1981, the Hengerer's name was no longer, officially becoming just Sibley's.[546]

That same day, Buffalo's largest local store, AM&A's, took out large newspaper ads "welcoming" Sibley's to Buffalo as if it was brand new to the market. Sibley's management was less than pleased with the ads, but in the end their fates would be nearly identical.[547]

In late 1982, Sibley's surveyed Buffalo to consider adding a sixth store to the market, but it never materialized.[548] It did add a store at the Boulevard Mall in 1983 in the former Sattler's space. In October 1986,

Associated Dry Goods merged with May Department Stores in a $2.47 billion sale.[549]

Rumors of the sale of Buffalo's downtown Sibley's store were acknowledged in February 1987. "The downtown Buffalo store has had a steady decline in sales for several years," said James Abrams of May Department Stores.[550] Just a week later, it announced the closing of the store, effective March 31.[551] May Department Stores said that it was an underperforming store, and everyone, from employees to politicians, had a reason for its decline.

Buffalo News reporter Jerry Zremski summed it up nicely: "Behind the Sibley's logo [on the Main Street store] the words 'Wm. Hengerer Co.' are spelled out in stains." Sibley's didn't even bother to clean the store's façade when it took over.[552] The building was sold in late 1987 and after renovations became office space,[553] and by the end of 1989, it was nearly full.

In 1988, Sibley's was the first store to open at the under-construction megamall Walden Galleria in Cheektowaga. In 1989, it opened a location at McKinley Mall in Blasdell.

Rochester was unfortunate enough to experience Buffalo's pain when May announced that it would close the flagship Sibley's store in downtown Rochester.[554] Buffalo and Rochester weren't the only victims of the conglomeration, but the pain of losing such a large part of your community's heritage hurts regardless.

In February 1990, another change was in store for the Sibley's chain when parent company May Department Stores decided to merge Sibley's into its Kaufmann's chain.[555] Buffalo had only four stores left. That merger would last until September 2006, when Kaufmann's was merged with another May chain, Macy's.

The younger generation that grew up with malls, the Internet and chain stores will never completely understand, or have the same attachment for, a store like older generations once did. The one positive note was that Hengerer's didn't end up bankrupt like many other Buffalo stores did, and several are still open.

Year founded: 1836
Year closed: 1981 (still open as Macy's)

OTHER LOCAL STORES

Conrad O. Machemer was a store clerk, working his way to Barnes, Bancroft & Company by 1877. The following year, he opened his own store at 224 William Street selling "dry goods and notions."[556] By 1892, his merchandise mix changed to "dry goods, carpets, and varieties," and he moved to 211–215 William Street. In 1904, the city directory listing changed to Catharine Machemer (his wife), "dry goods," and in 1906 to Machemer's Dry Goods Store. In 1909, George L. Arms joined the firm, and it became Machemer & Arms Company, a department store. Arms left, and the name was changed to Machemer Company and then to Machemer Bros. Department Store; finally, by 1917, it was gone. Machemer's son William, who had been running it at the end, found work as a superintendent in a knitting mill.

Margaret Marchand came to Buffalo as a child from Nuremberg, Germany. When her husband, John, died in 1873, she decided to open a store to support her young family. The variety store was opened in 1875 at 757 Michigan Avenue and did remarkably well. By 1899, her sons were full-time employees, and the company was renamed M. Marchand & Sons—dry goods and shoes. The continued success afforded them the ability to open a warehouse at 28–30 Cherry Street and a location at 21 Court Street in 1925. By 1930, the store was closed. Son Andrew continued in the dry goods business several years later, opening his own store. Mrs. Marchand was recognized as a pioneer in the dry goods business in Buffalo.[557]

One store that was able to survive longer than most of its peers was Jenss. This store was started in Lockport, New York, by the Jenss brothers in 1887. It went on to buy the former Zuckmaier Brothers department store in Tonawanda and opened a branch in the Eastern Hills Mall. In 1951, Harold Dautch bought the company and together with a group of local investors built the Boulevard Mall, where Jenss built its flagship store. On September 15, 2000, the company ended the local department store era in Western New York when it closed its doors. The company had a partnership with Reeds Jewelers that it continued after the closing with Reeds Jenss, a jewelry and gift chain.

Shopping Plazas and Malls

Downtown is the hub of retailing in Western New York. For the customer, it represents the most effective shopping experience, and it's exciting to see the vitality so evident in the Downtown area.[558]
—Stan L. Smolen, president, the Kleinhans Company, 1976

They were both the detriment and at the same time the future of retailing, not just in Buffalo but in cities across the country. Although Buffalo's population continued to grow until the late 1950s, after World War II, the population exodus to the suburbs was in full swing. As the population moved, the stores followed, until the stores were located in plazas and then malls, leaving downtown and Broadway-Fillmore in their dust. There was no going back. The following is a brief list of the major plazas and malls with a very brief history.

The University Plaza began construction in 1939 and opened on Main Street across from the University at Buffalo in about 1941. It was the first shopping center of its kind in Buffalo. AM&A's was one of the first tenants. Like all shopping centers, it has experienced ups and downs, but its location has allowed it to continue in operation at near capacity today.

Langfield Plaza, located at 2863 Bailey Avenue in Buffalo, opened in about 1947. One of the first tenants was E.W. Edwards.

The Sheridan Plaza, Sheridan Drive at Delaware Road, Tonawanda, opened in about 1949. AM&A's was an early tenant, and L.L. Berger added a store later.

The Airport Plaza opened in 1949 in Cheektowaga at Union and Genesee Streets, down the street from the Buffalo airport. Early tenants included AM&A's, Robert Hall's, Loblaws and an A&P grocery.

The L.B. Smith Plaza at 1234 Abbott Road in Lackawanna at the Buffalo city line opened in October 1951. Early tenants included E.W. Edwards, Hens & Kelly and AM&A's. After losing its major anchors, the plaza was able to survive with new tenants and is still viable today.

Thruway Plaza opened for business on October 16, 1952, at Walden Avenue and Harlem Road in Cheektowaga. It was built for $7 million and encompassed 300,000 leasable square feet. Originally open-air, the strip-type complex occupied a seventy-five-acre site. The structure was expanded with a two-block group of stores, fronting on a new open-air mall, in the mid-1950s. Early tenants included L.L. Berger; Oppenheim, Collins; H. Seeberg's; and A. Victor's. AM&A's built an anchor store that was completed in 1967, and ten years later, the shopping center was enlarged and enclosed, becoming Thruway Mall. Business declined after the Seneca and McKinley Malls opened, but when the Galleria Mall (located just a mile away) opened, the death warrant was signed. Stores shut down in record numbers, and most of the mall was demolished and returned to its original state as a plaza once again.

The Southgate Plaza on Union Road in West Seneca was constructed in 1954 and owned by the Lambein family until early 2013, when it was bought by Southgate Associates, LLC. Early tenants include AM&A's, Kobacker's, Krasner's and Nu-Way. The AM&A's location is still occupied by Bon-Ton.

Central Park Plaza opened in 1958 in a prime residential area in northeast Buffalo, a few blocks from Main and Amherst Streets but off any major road, which nearly doomed it from the start. "At its peak in the mid-1970s, Central Park Plaza included a Twin Fair, Tops, Super Duper, Bells, Nu-Way, S.S. Kresge, G.C. Murphy, Western Auto, several bank branches, and locations of several local retail chains."[559] By the late 1980s, the surrounding neighborhood demographics were changing, and stores started closing. Today, it is an empty plaza.

The Boulevard Mall on Niagara Falls Boulevard opened in 1962 in the Amherst/Tonawanda area. The anchor stores were J.C. Penney, Kobacker's and Jenss. Kobacker's and Jenss both closed, and Sibley's moved into Kobacker's location in 1983; it then became Kaufmann's and today is Macy's. The mall struggled after the Galleria opened but is doing well today.

The Main Place Mall opened in 1968 as part of a downtown renewal effort and a means to add more office and retail space to the downtown business district. The mall was located on the site of the former AM&A's

store. It was once anchored by Kobacker's, which later changed to Sattler's after Kobacker's closed, but that space was turned into a food court on the upper level, with more stores on the lower level.[560] The mall has become primarily office space over the years, with just a handful of stores still open.

When the Seneca Mall opened on Slade Avenue in 1969, it served the West Seneca/Orchard Park area. The anchor stores were J.C. Penney, Sattler's and Hengerer's. The Hengerer's store had a restaurant upstairs that overlooked the mall and was a popular spot for breakfast with Santa. From there, you could see the big, round fireplace that was in the center of the mall in front of Sattler's until it closed in 1982. The mall started to slide downhill at this time, and when McKinley Mall opened in 1985, some stores moved, including Hengerer's, which was now Sibley's, leaving just J.C. Penney. The Galleria Mall opened in 1989, and that sounded the death knell. The Galleria's owners, Pyramid, supposedly lured J.C. Penney by buying out its lease. In less than two years, the mall was dead. It sat empty until 1999 and was demolished,[561] with grand plans to open a large plaza. Several occupied stores stand where a large plaza was supposed to develop, but it never materialized.

The Eastern Hills Mall was opened in 1971 by the Edward J. DeBartolo Corporation of Cleveland on Transit Road in Clarence, New York, as the area's fourth and largest mall. Anchors at the time of opening were AM&A's, J.C. Penney, Sears, Jenss, Woolworth's and Hengerer's. The mall had full-scale carpeting throughout and outlandish center court designs. It was also equipped with a fountain and a General Cinema three-screen theater.[562] Multiple stores went out of business over the years, but they have been able to bring in new tenants and continue to operate.

The Como Mall was located on Union Road in Cheektowaga. In the 1970s, the small mall was anchored by Hens & Kelly, Century Housewares and the Como 8 theaters. It struggled for years as the anchors closed, and the mall was sold in 1984. When the Galleria opened, it killed any chance of growth. It was re-branded as the Appletree Mall and is now a business park.

McKinley Mall opened in 1985 on McKinley Parkway in Blasdell. It proved to be the Seneca Mall's biggest competitor, siphoning customers from the mall. AM&A's was the original anchor store. It also struggled when the Walden Galleria opened but has since added a Barnes & Noble and other stores.

The largest mall in Western New York opened in 1989. The Walden Galleria on Walden Avenue in Cheektowaga drove the stake into the Thruway and Seneca Malls and probably contributed to the decline of most of the other malls. Three local anchors included Sibley's, L.L. Berger and the Sample. The mall is still the largest in the area and has expanded several times since its opening.

Epilogue

She was the grande dame of Buffalo department stores, and she finally went down in dignity. It had crossed the tracks; its customers hadn't.[563]
—*writer Ray Hill commenting on Sattler's closing at Boulevard Mall*

Buffalo's great retailing past was both interesting and sad to write about. I couldn't help but see the same patterns replayed over and over and wonder what would have happened if it all played out differently.

What if Sattler's stayed in the family, kept its promotional style over the years and didn't try to be another upscale department store? New generations might have flocked to the store, and the Broadway-Fillmore neighborhood may not have declined like it did. At the same time, even if the neighborhood did decline, Sattler's may have stayed a viable shopping destination because of its product mix and buying power.

What if the stores didn't branch out to the suburbs and instead invested in their flagship stores? Would downtown have lost all of its luster?

What if the city never built the pedestrian mall and rapid transit? The years of construction killed some businesses and hastened the decline of others. L.L. Berger barely held on during the construction. Some cities tore out their pedestrian malls years ago. Buffalo's has been relatively popular over the years, especially Fountain Plaza. And now the city is starting to bring traffic back to Main Street.

What if the University at Buffalo had built its new campus downtown instead of the suburbs?

There are a lot of "what ifs," and no one will ever know what *could* have been. We only know what was and what is.

In 1990, the *Buffalo News* printed an interesting analysis regarding store closings throughout the years that were followed by recessions. In 1952, E.W. Edwards closed, followed by a ten-month recession in July 1953.

In 1956, Flint & Kent closed, and in August 1957, an eight-month recession began. In 1959, J.N. Adam closed, followed in April 1960 by a ten-month recession. In 1972, Kobacker's closed, and in November 1973, an eleven-month recession began.

In 1981, Hens & Kelly closed, and in 1982, Twin Fair and Sattler's both closed. There was a six-month recession in early 1980, followed by a sixteen-month recession that began in July 1981.

Of those closures, three stores weren't locally owned. Although it wasn't a scientific study, it does show an interesting pattern. For the most part, it seems that the stores' sales forecast the decline of the economy. After all, they were one of the first places consumers would abandon when finances were tight. No new furniture, appliances, housewares, clothing—just the necessities.

The retail scene in Buffalo is far different than it was fifty years ago. Downtown has several small clothing and variety stores, as well as national drugstores. The Main Place Mall, originally thought to be a savior for downtown, is nearly empty. Main Street is starting to see a rebirth, and the City of Buffalo is tearing out the pedestrian mall, block by block, and returning traffic to Main Street.

The Broadway-Fillmore area is also vastly different. The big stores like Sattler's, Kobacker's and Posmantur's have given way to rent-to-own chains, dollar stores and fast-food restaurants.

Other neighborhood shopping districts once popular for chain stores like Grant-Ferry, Riverside, Kensington-Bailey, Jefferson and Seneca Street still survive, but they are all much different; most are struggling.

Elmwood and Hertel Avenues have become the new breeding grounds for retailing in Buffalo, attracting an ever-expanding variety of stores and restaurants—mostly homegrown, but even some chains have found homes there. The suburban malls continue to evolve, and the Galleria is constantly expanding and remodeling to stay on top.

The department stores, the malls, the neighborhood commercial districts, shopping downtown or taking the bus to Sattler's will forever be in our memories, both their good and bad aspects, and they will always allow us to relive a time when Buffalo was king and we were innocent.

Notes

Preface

1. *New York Times*, October 2, 1992, D3.
2. *Buffalo News*, February 1, 1906, A9.

Introduction

3. See McGarry, *University of Buffalo Studies in Business*.

Chain Stores

4. Darby, *Story of the Chain Store*, 82.
5. Ibid.
6. Wikipedia, "Kmart Corporation," http://en.wikipedia.org/wiki/Kmart_Corporation.
7. Ibid.

8. *New York Times*, April 4, 1987, 33.

9. *Buffalo Evening News*, November 3, 1966, 57.

10. Ibid., May 8, 1967, 16.

11. Ibid., April 11, 1969.

12. *Courier Express*, December 2, 1977, 19.

13. Ibid., January 10, 1978, 6.

14. Ibid., November August 1978, 16.

15. Old Newark Memories, "Two Guys from Harrison," http://www.oldnewark. com/memories/newark/newmantwoguys.htm.

16. Wikipedia, "Blue law," http://en.wikipedia.org/wiki/Blue_law.

17. *New York Times*, April 2, 1986, B6.

18. Ibid., February 9, 1982.

19. *Buffalo Evening News*, April 15, 1976, 1.

20. Internet Archive Wayback Machine, "King's Department Store."

21. Wikipedia, "Hills Department Store," http://en.wikipedia.org/wiki/Hills_Department_Store.

22. Ibid., "Ames," http://en.wikipedia.org/wiki/Ames.

23. Controlled-Demolition, Inc., "J.L. Hudson Department Store," http://www.controlled-demolition.com/jl-hudson-department-store.

24. *Courier Express*, October 5, 1929, 20.

25. Ibid., November 20, 1949, 5, 9.

26. Ibid., September 16, 1951, 2, 5.

27. National Museum of American History, "Jane Parker Cake Advertising Sample Book, 1947," http://americanhistory.si.edu/archives/d7720.htm.

28. Wikipedia, "The Great Atlantic & Pacific Tea Company," http://en.wikipedia.org/wiki/The_Great_Atlantic_and_Pacific_Tea_Company.

29. *Courier Express*, July 19, 1953, 30A.

30. Ibid.

31. Internet Archive Wayback Machine, "A&P's History," Great Atlantic & Pacific Tea Company.

32. *Buffalo Evening News*, April 10, 1975, 1.

33. Great Atlantic & Pacific Tea Company, "Our Company," http://aptea.com/our-company.

34. Wikipedia, "W.T. Grant," http://en.wikipedia.org/wiki/WT_Grant.

35. *Courier Express*, May 19, 1928, 22.

36. *Industry in Buffalo Scrapbook*, vol. 4, 359.

37. *Buffalo Evening News*, March 24, 1966, 1.

38. Wikipedia, "W.T. Grant."

39. *Buffalo Evening News*, August 11, 1966, 35.

40. Gary H. Scott correspondence with author.

41. *Buffalo Express*, May 16, 1925, 12.

42. Ibid.

43. *Industry in Buffalo Scrapbook*, vol. 3, 197.

44. Ibid., vol. 4, 312.

45. *Courier Express*, December 21, 1940, 10.

46. Ibid., November 24, 1945, 14.

47. Ibid., April 13, 1947, sec. 5, 7.

48. Ibid., June 22, 1947, sec. 5, 1.

49. Ibid., August 13, 1950, sec. 6, 5.

50. Ibid., October 5, 1951, 13.

51. Ibid., August 15, 1952, 1.

52. Ibid.

53. *Industry in Buffalo Scrapbook*, vol. 7, 249.

54. *Courier Express*, March 5, 1954, 21.

55. Ibid., June 17, 1977, 19.

56. *New York Times*, "David Weisz, 70, Auctioneer of Shipyards and Movie Sets," July 1, 1981, http://query.nytimes.com/gst/fullpage.html?res=9D02E1D61138 F932A35754C0A967948260.

57. *Courier Express*, May 7, 1937, sec. 8, 9.

58. *Industry in Buffalo Scrapbook*, vol. 3, 505.

59. Ibid., vol. 9, 27.

Discount Stores

60. Louise Seibold correspondence with author.

61. Buffalo and Erie County Public Library, *Local Biographies Scrapbook* (hereafter *Local Biographies*), vol. 19, 203–4.

62. *Industry in Buffalo Scrapbook*, vol. 3, 339.

63. *Local Biographies*, vol. 19, 204.

64. *Industry in Buffalo Scrapbook*, vol. 3, 339.

65. Ibid.

66. Ibid.

67. Ibid., vol. 1, 340.

68. *Local Biographies*, vol. 19, 204.

69. *Buffalo Evening News*, April 12, 1939.

70. Wikipedia, "F.W. Woolworth Company," http://en.wikipedia.org/wiki/F.W._Woolworth_Company.

71. Ibid.

72. *New York Times,* July 18, 1997, A1.

73. Wikipedia, "F.W. Woolworth Company."

74. *Buffalo Magazine* (March 1965): 42.

75. Ibid.

76. *Industry in Buffalo Scrapbook,* vol. 9, 76.

77. *Buffalo Magazine* (March 1965): 42.

78. Ibid.

79. Ibid.

80. Ibid.

81. Ibid.

82. *New York Times,* March 27, 1982, 30.

83. *Buffalo Evening News,* September 7, 1988, 1.

CLOTHING AND JEWELRY STORES

84. *Courier Express,* September 12, 1976, 37.

85. *Buffalo News,* April 20, 2004.

86. Buffalo City Directory, 1950.

87. *Buffalo News,* April 20, 2004.

88. *Buffalo Evening News,* June 18, 1991, B7.

89. *Buffalo Express,* May 9, 1926, 8, 9.

90. *Courier Express,* February 5, 1944, 6.

91. *Buffalo News,* September 24, 1992, A1.

92. Ibid., September 25, 1992, B7.

93. *New York Times,* October 2, 1992, D3.

94. *Courier Express,* April 20, 1975, advertisement.

95. Ibid., February 5, 1928.

96. Ibid., April 20, 1975, magazine.

97. Ibid., February 5, 1928, 9.

98. Ibid.

99. Ibid.

100. Ibid.

101. *Industry in Buffalo Scrapbook,* vol. 40.

102. *Courier Express*, September 6, 1942, sec. 5, 2.

103. Ibid., June 14, 1944, 11.

104. Ibid., January 5, 1945, 11.

105. *Industry in Buffalo Scrapbook*, vol. 8, 208.

106. *Buffalo Evening News*, May 28, 1949.

107. Marcia and Marvin Frankel correspondence with author, July 8, 2013.

108. *Courier Express*, August 2, 1953, B1.

109. Ibid., August 16, 1973.

110. *Buffalo Evening News*, January 2, 1958, 25.

111. *Industry in Buffalo Scrapbook*, vol. 9, 10.

112. *Courier Express*, April 25, 1962, 29.

113. Ibid., June 26, 1967.

114. *Buffalo Evening News*, March 3, 1999, A6.

115. Ibid., February 8, 2002.

116. *Courier Express*, August 11, 1968, 22.

117. Marcia and Marvin Frankel correspondence with author, July 8, 2013.

118. *Courier Express*, February 25, 1979.

119. *Buffalo Evening News*, August 27, 1980, 19.

120. Ibid., May 30, 1990.

121. Ibid., January 14, 1991, A1.

122. Ibid.

123. Ibid.

124. Ibid., February 6, 1991, A1.

125. *Buffalo News*, February 5, 1995, B11.

126. *Buffalo Evening News*, February 7, 1991, A1.

127. Ibid., March 27, 1994.

128. Ibid., February 7, 1991, A1.

129. Marcia and Marvin Frankel correspondence with author, July 8, 2013.

130. Ibid.

131. *Industry in Buffalo Scrapbook*, vol. 4, 337.

132. Ibid.

133. *Courier Express*, February 9, 1968, 5.

134. Erie County Clerk Office (ECCO) business certificate records, 1928.

135. *Industry in Buffalo Scrapbook*, vol. 7, 277.

136. *Buffalo Evening News*, August 26, 1989, A7.

137. *Industry in Buffalo Scrapbook*, vol. 7, 277.

138. *Courier Express*, March 31, 1946, sec. 7, 1.

139. Ibid.

140. *Industry in Buffalo Scrapbook*, vol. 12, 77.

141. David Bunis correspondence with author, August 7, 2013.

142. Ibid.

143. *Industry in Buffalo Scrapbook*, vol. 9, 8.

144. David Bunis correspondence with author, August 7, 2013.

145. *Buffalo Evening News*, August 26, 1989, A7.

146. David Bunis correspondence with author, August 7, 2013.

147. *Buffalo Evening News*, October 19, 1989, C9.

148. Ibid., November 30, 1989, D5.

149. David Bunis correspondence with author, August 7, 2013.

150. *Buffalo Evening News*, March 14, 1990, C5.

151. David Bunis correspondence with author, August 7, 2013.

152. *Buffalo Evening News*, September 13, 1990, D7.

153. Ibid., October 15, 1990, A1.

154. Ibid., January 20, 1993, 3C.

155. Ibid.

156. Ibid., June 29, 1999, C6.

157. Ibid., September 29, 1964, 20.

158. *Courier Express*, February 22, 1941, 15.

159. Ibid.

160. Mueller, *Buffalo and Its German Community*, 204–5.

161. Buffalo City Directory, 1903.

162. Mueller, *Buffalo and Its German Community*, 204–5.

163. Bailey, *Illustrated Buffalo*, 162.

164. Online Archive of California, "Inventory of Peter Young Lantern Slides of America," http://www.oac.cdlib.org/findaid/ark:/13030/c8bk1d35/entire_text.

165. Buffalo City Directory, 1903.

166. *Courier Express*, September 24, 1950, 7D.

167. Buffalo City Directory, 1916.

168. *Courier Express*, September 24, 1950, 7D.

169. Ibid., June 28, 1962, 4.

170. *Industry in Buffalo Scrapbook*, vol. 9, 139.

171. Riverside Men's Shop, "Store History of Riverside Men's Shop," http://www.riversidemens.com/store-history.html.

172. *Buffalo News*, November 24, 2006, D6.

173. *Courier Express*, October 2, 1975, 26.

174. *Buffalo Evening News*, December 1, 1997, C1.

175. Ibid., July 30, 1968, 33.

176. Ibid., October 28, 1989, obit.

177. Ibid., December 31, 1994, A5.
178. Ibid., December 1, 1997, C1.

GROCERY STORES AND DRUGSTORES

179. *Buffalo Evening News*, February 6, 1991, A1.
180. *Local Biographies*, series 3, vol. 1, 203–4.
181. Buffalo City Directory, 1899.
182. *Local Biographies*, series 3, vol. 1, 203–4.
183. *Buffalo Daily Courier*, February 25, 1920, 2.
184. *Courier Express*, July 4, 1928, 24.
185. Buffalo Architecture and History, "John D. Larkin and the Larkin Company," http://www.buffaloah.com/h/jw/larkin.html.
186. *Industry in Buffalo Scrapbook*, vol. 4; *Buffalo Evening News*, May 6, 1937.
187. *Courier Express*, July 11, 1980, 15.
188. Ibid., July 4, 1979, 3.
189. Rizzo, *Through the Mayors' Eyes*, 122.
190. *Industry in Buffalo Scrapbook*, vol. 28, 4.
191. *Courier Express*, June 11, 1944, 5, 7.
192. Ibid., July 9, 1972, 32.
193. Ibid.
194. Ibid.
195. Wikipedia, "George Weston," http://en.wikipedia.org/wiki/George_Weston.
196. *Buffalo Evening News*, February 5, 1989, B12.
197. Ibid., May 21, 1974, 52.
198. *Courier Express*, May 9, 1954, 3B.
199. Ibid., March 20, 1965, 21.
200. *Buffalo Evening News*, May 21, 1974, 52.
201. Ibid., February 5, 1989, B12.
202. Ibid., May 29, 1992, A1.
203. Ibid.
204. *Business First*, January 11, 1993.
205. *Supermarket News*, October 1994.
206. Ibid., May 1993.
207. *Local Biographies*, vol. 12, 36–39.
208. Ibid.

209. *Industry in Buffalo Scrapbook*, vol. 7, 21.

210. *Courier Express*, March 28, 1978, 21.

211. *Buffalo News*, November 4, 1991, A9.

212. *New York Times*, July 2, 1994, 33.

213. *Courier Express*, February 25, 1968, 55.

214. Ibid.

215. *Buffalo Evening News*, June 7, 2000, D8.

216. *Courier Express*, January 4, 1976, 34.

217. ECCO corporation records, Tops.

218. Wikipedia, "Tops Friendly Markets," http://en.wikipedia.org/wiki/Tops_Friendly_Markets.

219. Ibid.

220. *New York Times*, February 28, 1991, D4.

221. Tops Friendly Markets website.

222. *Business First*, May 5, 2003.

223. *New York Times*, May 27, 2003, C4.

224. *Business First*, June 20, 2005.

225. *Buffalo News*, October 12, 2007, A1.

226. Ibid., May 15, 2010, D7.

227. *Local History Scrapbook*, vol. 2, 364.

228. *Binghamton Express*, May 17, 1929, 19.

229. *Niagara Falls Gazette*, July 29, 1926, 16.

230. *Industry in Buffalo Scrapbook*, vol. 3, 236.

231. River Campus Libraries, "Bristol, Cyrenius C."

232. See Shaw, *History of the Comstock Patent Medicine Business*.

233. *Courier Express*, December 16, 1948, 10.

234. Wikipedia, "Fay's Drug: Beginning," http://en.wikipedia.org/wiki/Fay%27s_Drugs#Beginning.

Hardware and Home Furnishings

235. MP3 Trusts, "Gene Wisniewski Urban Lucki Jingles," http://mp3trusts.com/index.php?q=wisniewski+gene+lucki+urban+jingles+master+reel+copy+c+1&type=mp3.

236. Buffalo Historical Society, *Publications of the Buffalo Historical Society*, vol. 16, 409.

237. Western New York Heritage Press, "Denton & Co.," http://wnyheritagepress.org/features/denton.htm.

238. Archivaria, "The Magnificent Success of a Firm."

239. Denton, Cotter & Daniels Pianos & Organs, "About Our Company," http://www.dentoncottieranddaniels.com/about.htm.

240. Bailey, *Illustrated Buffalo*, 105.

241. *Buffalo Evening News*, January 11, 2002.

242. Ibid., July 22, 1947.

243. John Henrich Company Inc., "About Us," http://johnhenrich.com/about.

244. Ibid.

245. Ibid.

246. Ibid.

247. Ibid.

248. *Buffalo Times*, February 8, 1923.

249. *Local Biographies*, series 2, vol. 4, 246.

250. Ibid.

251. Mueller, *Buffalo and Its German Community*, 204–5.

252. Ibid.

253. Rizzo, *Through the Mayors' Eyes*, 217.

254. *Buffalo Evening News*, May 17, 1946, 16.

255. Ibid., January 25, 1989, C6.

256. Ibid.

257. *Industry in Buffalo Scrapbook*, vol. 3, 508.

258. *Buffalo Times*, July 31, 1909, 4.

259. Bailey, *Illustrated Buffalo*, 100.

260. *Industry in Buffalo Scrapbook*, vol. 3, 509.

261. *Buffalo Times*, July 31, 1909, 4.

262. *Industry in Buffalo Scrapbook*, vol. 3, 510.

263. *Local Biographies*, series 6, vol. 3, 183–84.

264. Ibid.

265. *Industry in Buffalo Scrapbook*, vol. 3, 493.

266. Ibid., 498.

267. Ibid., 504.

268. *Buffalo Express*, April 4, 1926, 1, 8.

269. *Industry in Buffalo Scrapbook*, vol. 3, 504.

270. Ibid., vol. 6, 81.

271. *Buffalo Evening News*, January 11, 1956, 1.

272. Ibid., September 1, 1959, 1.

273. *Industry in Buffalo Scrapbook*, vol. 9, 231.

274. *Buffalo Evening News*, November 20, 1963, 55.

275. *Local Biographies*, series 4, vol. 2, 221.

276. *New York Times*, August 2, 1956, 35.

277. *Buffalo Evening News*, July 12, 1968, 19.

278. *Buffalo News*, June 12, 2000, C1.

279. Ibid., June 28, 1992, B23.

280. Ibid., January 7, 1998, B6.

281. Ibid., June 3, 1997, D3.

282. *Industry in Buffalo Scrapbook*, vol. 4, 37.

283. Ibid., vol. 6, 126.

284. Ibid.; *Buffalo Evening News*, October 17, 1945.

285. *Buffalo Evening News*, March 18, 2001, B13.

286. See the *1973 Century Housewares Catalogue*, headquarters in Orchard Park, New York.

287. Bailey, *Illustrated Buffalo*, 108.

288. Ibid.

289. Buffalo City Directory, 1887.

290. *Buffalo Evening News*, January 12, 2003, C9.

291. Ibid., March 4, 1994, B6.

Department Stores

292. Bills Backers United, "History of Pro Football in Western New York."

293. *Courier Express*, January 14, 1940, sec. 5, 5.

294. Ibid.

295. Ibid., August 21, 1941, 24.

296. See *AM&A's: Adam, Meldrum & Anderson Co, 100 Years*.

297. Ibid.

298. Ibid.

299. *Courier Express*, March 19, 1967.

300. See *AM&A's: Adam, Meldrum & Anderson Co, 100 Years*.

301. *Buffalo Daily Courier*, 1874.

302. *Buffalo Express*, September 1888.

303. Business History Books, "Industries: Business History of Utilities."

304. *Industry in Buffalo Scrapbook*, vol. 4, 264.

305. Ibid., 295.

306. Ross, *Scot in America*, 266.

307. *Buffalo Magazine* (March 1966): 20–22.

308. See *AM&A's: Adam, Meldrum & Anderson Co, 100 Years*.

309. *Buffalo Express*, April 29, 1925, 9.

310. *Industry in Buffalo Scrapbook*, vol. 3, 13.

311. Ibid.

312. Ibid., 145.

313. *Buffalo Evening News*, November 21, 1932, 3.

314. *Buffalo News*, April 9, 1989, B15.

315. *Buffalo Evening News*, May 5, 1947, 1.

316. *Courier Express*, July 19, 1947, 4.

317. *Buffalo News*, August 30, 1994, 36.

318. *Industry in Buffalo Scrapbook*, vol. 9, 71.

319. Ibid.

320. See *AM&A's: Adam, Meldrum & Anderson Co, 100 Years.*

321. *Buffalo Evening News*, July 27, 1963, A4.

322. Ibid., January 18, 1964, C4.

323. *Industry in Buffalo Scrapbook*, vol. 10, 66.

324. Ibid., 54.

325. *Buffalo Evening News*, October 30, 1964, 29.

326. *Courier Express*, October 31, 1964, 3.

327. *Buffalo Evening News*, March 11, 1966, 31.

328. *Courier Express*, March 4, 1966, 17.

329. *Buffalo Evening News*, September 25, 1967, 25.

330. *Courier Express*, June 27, 1969, 30.

331. Department Store Museum, "AM&A's," http://departmentstoremuseum. blogspot.com/2010/11/adam-meldrum-anderson-co-buffalo-new.html.

332. *Buffalo Evening News*, November 26, 1969, 70.

333. Ibid., July 31, 1970, 19.

334. *Courier Express*, August 7, 1971, 5.

335. *Buffalo Evening News*, August 6, 1971, 15.

336. *Courier Express*, February 13, 1972, 6.

337. *Buffalo Evening News*, September 5, 1974, 38.

338. *Courier Express*, November 26, 1976, 4.

339. *Buffalo News*, April 9, 1989, B15.

340. Ibid.

341. Ibid., July 6, 1990, B7.

342. Ibid., August 9, 1993, A9.

343. Ibid., September 12, 1993, obit.

344. Ibid., May 6, 1994, A1.

345. Ibid., May 8, 1994, B13.

346. Ibid.

347. Ibid., July 12, 1994, B7.

348. Ibid., July 6, 1994, C3.

349. Ibid., September 23, 1994, A9.

350. Ibid., January 10, 1995, A1.

351. Ibid., February 3, 1995, A1.

352. Ibid., March 21, 1995, A5.

353. Ibid., June 12, 1999, A1.

354. *Industry in Buffalo Scrapbook*, vol. 9, 284.

355. Ibid., 285.

356. IEEE Global History Network, "Early Electrification of Buffalo."

357. *Industry in Buffalo Scrapbook*, vol. 9, 286.

358. Rizzo, *Through the Mayors' Eyes*.

359. *Buffalo Express*, March 18, 1905.

360. *New York Times*, May 26, 1909, 5.

361. Wikipedia, "Associated Dry Goods," http://en.wikipedia.org/wiki/Associated_Dry_Goods.

362. Rizzo, *Through the Mayors' Eyes*.

363. *Industry in Buffalo Scrapbook*, vol. 3, 6.

364. Ibid., vol. 9, 287.

365. Ibid., vol. 4, 295.

366. Ibid., 296.

367. Ibid., vol. 6, 101.

368. Ibid., vol. 7, 6.

369. Ibid., 66.

370. *Courier Express*, May 23, 1943, sec. 4, 10.

371. Ibid., February 26, 1949, 15.

372. *Industry in Buffalo Scrapbook*, vol. 9, 74.

373. *New York Times*, July 17, 1986.

374. *Courier Express*, June 21, 1941, 24.

375. *Industry in Buffalo Scrapbook*, vol. 5, 121.

376. Hill, *Municipality of Buffalo*, vol. 4, 441.

377. Ibid.

378. Ibid.

379. *Buffalo Times*, December 15, 1928.

380. *Courier Express*, June 13, 1929, 9; February 28, 1932, sec. 9, 4.

381. Encyclopedia Titanica, "Mr. Edward Austin Kent."

382. *Industry in Buffalo Scrapbook*, vol. 3, 225.

383. Ibid., 227.

384. Ibid., vol. 9, 13; *Buffalo Evening News*, February 26, 1959.

385. *Industry in Buffalo Scrapbook*, vol. 10, 300; *Buffalo Evening News*, February 2, 1946, 41.

386. Mary Hoffman correspondence with author.

387. *Buffalo Evening News*, September 22, 1897, 3.

388. National Park Service, "H.A. Meldrum Company Building."

389. *Buffalo Express*, 1901, 4.

390. *Industry in Buffalo Scrapbook*, vol. 3, 443.

391. *Buffalo Evening News*, January 22, 1913, 15.

392. *Buffalo Express*, May 7, 1913, 6.

393. *Buffalo Courier*, October 19, 1913, 88.

394. *Buffalo Evening News*, November 6, 1916, 7.

395. See the 1900 U.S. Census.

396. *Local Biographies*, series 3, vol. 1, 286.

397. Ibid., series 1, vol. 18, 254.

398. *Buffalo Evening News*, January 6, 1898, 5.

399. *Local Biographies*, series 3, vol. 1, 286.

400. Ibid., series 1, vol. 18, 254.

401. *Industry in Buffalo Scrapbook*, vol. 3, 300.

402. Ibid.

403. *Local Biographies*, series 1, vol. 18, 254.

404. *New York Times*, April 9, 1928, 3.

405. *Industry in Buffalo Scrapbook*, vol. 9, 45.

406. Ibid.

407. Ibid., 108.

408. Personal collection of David Hens.

409. *Courier Express*, June 2, 1978, 39.

410. *Buffalo Evening News*, February 14, 1982, 25.

411. Ibid.

412. Ibid., December 1, 1982, B14.

413. *Buffalo News*, November 14, 2007, B3.

414. Ibid., June 21, 1939.

415. *Buffalo Courier*, March 1, 1898, 7.

416. Ibid., 1904.

417. Ibid.

418. *Lockport Journal*, February 27, 1904.

419. *Buffalo and Its Points of Interest*, 65.

420. Ibid.

421. Matthews, *Men of New York*, vol. 1, 144–45.

422. Ibid.

423. Ibid.

424. *Industry in Buffalo Scrapbook*, vol. 4, 305–9.

425. Ibid.

426. Ibid.

427. Ibid., 305.

428. Ibid.

429. *Courier Express*, October 5, 1938, 22.

430. *Industry in Buffalo Scrapbook*, vol. 4, 305.

431. *Buffalo Evening News*, April 9, 1963, 21.

432. Ibid., August 1, 1963, 10.

433. *Industry in Buffalo Scrapbook*, vol. 10, 74.

434. Ibid.

435. Ibid.

436. Ibid.

437. Ibid.

438. *Coronet Magazine* (October 1948): 77–80.

439. Ibid.

440. *Courier Express*, August 4, 1979, 26.

441. Clark, *Brainstorming*.

442. *Courier Express*, August 4, 1979, 26.

443. Ibid., November 11, 1939, 15.

444. *Industry in Buffalo Scrapbook*, vol. 4, 16.

445. Ibid., vol. 5, 100.

446. *Courier Express*, December 29, 1945, 9.

447. Ibid., October 17, 1946, 32.

448. *Buffalo Evening News*, October 17, 1946, 32.

449. *Courier Express*, September 3, 1947, 18.

450. Ibid.

451. Ibid., September 5, 1947, 8.

452. Ibid., June 22, 1950, 21.

453. Ibid.

454. Ibid.

455. Ibid., April 5, 1953, sec. 6, 2.

456. *Buffalo Evening News*, August 14, 1953, 29.

457. *Courier Express*, June 30, 1953, 26.

458. *Industry in Buffalo Scrapbook*, vol. 4, 47.

459. *Courier Express*, July 17, 1957, 1.

460. Wayne State University Digital Collections, "Ernst Kern Co," http://dlxs.lib. wayne.edu/d/dhhcc/retailers/kern.html.

461. *Buffalo Evening News*, September 19, 1956, 7.

462. *Industry in Buffalo Scrapbook*, vol. 9, 70.

463. Ibid., 123.
464. *Buffalo Evening News*, July 10, 1961, 15.
465. Ibid., June 28, 1963, 19.
466. Ibid., January 4, 1964, 14.
467. *Courier Express*, December 27, 1964, 3; *Industry in Buffalo Scrapbook*, vol. 10, 19.
468. *Buffalo Evening News*, September 1, 1965, 62.
469. Ibid.
470. Ibid., April 22, 1966, 47.
471. *Courier Express*, August 21, 1968, 54.
472. *Buffalo Evening News*, August 28, 1968, 1.
473. Ibid., May 16, 1969, 21.
474. Ibid.
475. *Courier Express*, July 20, 1972, 5.
476. *Buffalo Evening News*, May 11, 1973, 39.
477. Ibid., July 26, 1976, 1.
478. Ibid., October 28, 1979, 36.
479. Ibid., October 12, 1978.
480. Ibid., March 8, 1978, 50.
481. Ibid., April 25, 1979, 53.
482. *Courier Express*, August 4, 1979, 26.
483. Ibid., August 7, 1980, B11.
484. Ibid., September 1, 1979, 26.
485. *Buffalo Evening News*, October 4, 1979, 40.
486. *Courier Express*, October 21, 1979, 12.
487. Ibid., January 25, 1980, 26.
488. Ibid., 1.
489. Ibid.
490. *Buffalo Evening News*, July 23, 1980, 26.
491. Ibid., September 30, 1980, 15.
492. Ibid., November 25, 1980, 1.
493. Ibid., January 30, 1981, 7.
494. *Courier Express*, January 30, 1981, 19.
495. Ibid., March 31, 1981, 29.
496. Ibid., April 1, 1981, 3.
497. Ibid., September 10, 1981, A3.
498. Ibid., November 24, 1981, 18.
499. *Buffalo Evening News*, January 25, 1982, 1.
500. Ibid., February 18, 1982, C12.
501. Ibid., December 19, 1982, D2.
502. Ibid., December 15, 1982, 1.

503. *Local Biographies*, series 2, vol. 6, 140.

504. Ibid.

505. *Buffalo Illustrated Express*, October 3, 1897, sec. 1, 8.

506. Ibid.

507. Ibid.

508. Ibid.

509. Ibid.

510. Ibid.

511. Ibid.

512. *Local Biographies*, vol. 15, 244–45.

513. *Industry in Buffalo Scrapbook*, vol. 3, 288.

514. Ibid., 286.

515. Ibid., 285.

516. Ibid., 291.

517. Ibid., 292.

518. *Local Biographies*, vol. 15, 246.

519. *Industry in Buffalo Scrapbook*, vol. 4, 117.

520. *Local Biographies*, vol. 15, 246.

521. *Courier Express*, December 29, 1935, sec. 7, 1.

522. Ibid., April 4, 1936, 16.

523. *Industry in Buffalo Scrapbook*, vol. 4, 315.

524. *Courier Express*, August 9, 1941, 18.

525. Ibid., January 3, 1946, 8.

526. Ibid., September 29, 1946, sec. 5, 5.

527. Ibid., August 14, 1947, 19.

528. Ibid., June 5, 1951, 14.

529. Ibid., July 1, 1951, 11.

530. Ibid., April 13, 1952, 28.

531. Department Store Museum, "Wm. Hengerer Co.," http://departmentstoremuseum.blogspot.com/2010/07/wm-hengerer-co-buffalo-new-york.html.

532. *Industry in Buffalo Scrapbook*, vol. 9, 72.

533. *Courier Express*, July 23, 1961, 18.

534. *Buffalo Evening News*, December 18, 1962, 12.

535. Ibid., September 27, 1963, 43.

536. Ibid., March 17, 1964, 46.

537. Ibid., April 1, 1969, 74.

538. *Courier Express*, August 3, 1971, 6; November 7, 1971, 4.

539. *Buffalo Evening News*, May 11, 1974, B5.

540. Ibid., September 13, 1976, 11.

541. Ibid., December 30, 1978, C2.

542. Ibid., January 29, 1981, 30.

543. *Courier Express*, January 30, 1981, 19.

544. *Buffalo Evening News*, June 5, 1981, 1.

545. Ibid., February 2, 1981, 1.

546. Ibid., October 30, 1981, 1.

547. *Courier Express*, November 15, 1981, C11.

548. *Buffalo Evening News*, October 13, 1982, A1.

549. *New York Times*, October 4, 1986, 32.

550. *Buffalo Evening News*, February 19, 1987, 8C.

551. Ibid., February 27, 1987, A1.

552. Ibid., March 1, 1987, B11.

553. Ibid., January 24, 1988, B1.

554. Ibid., January 30, 1990, C5.

555. Ibid., January 5, 1990, A1.

556. Buffalo City Directory, 1880.

557. *Local Biographies*, series 1, vol. 22, 180.

Shopping Plazas and Malls

558. *Courier Express*, February 1, 1976, supplement, 10.

559. Cyburgia, "Buffalo's Central Park Plaza: They Built a Shopping Center Where?," http://www.cyburbia.org/forums/showthread.php?t=48228.

560. Dead Malls, "Main Place Mall," http://deadmalls.com/malls/main_place_mall.html.

561. Ibid., "Seneca Mall," http://deadmalls.com/malls/seneca_mall.html.

562. Ibid., "Eastern Hills Mall," http://deadmalls.com/malls/eastern_hills_mall.html.

Epilogue

563. *Buffalo Evening News*, February 10, 1991.

Bibliography

BOOKS

Bailey, George M. *Illustrated Buffalo: The Queen City of the Lakes*. New York: Acme Publishing, 1896.

Beinecke, William Sperry. *Through Mem'ry's Haze: A Personal Memoir*. New York: Prospect Hill Press, 2000.

Birmingham, Nan Tillson. *Store*. New York: G.P. Putnam's Sons, 1978.

Buffalo and Its Points of Interest: Illustrated. New York: Commercial Pub. Company, 1896.

Buffalo Illustrated. Buffalo, NY: Courier Printing Company, 1890.

Clark, Charles H. *Brainstorming: The Dynamic New Way to Create Successful Ideas*. North Hollywood, CA: MeJvin Powers Wilshire Book Company, 1958. https://s3-eu-west-1.amazonaws.com/keyoflife2/Brainstorming.pdf.

Darby, W.D. *Story of the Chain Store*. New York: Dry Goods Economist, 1928.

Dunn, Walter S., Jr., ed. *History of Erie County, 1870–1970*. Buffalo, NY: Buffalo and Erie County Historical Society, 1972.

Elvins, Sarah. *Sales & Celebrations*. Athens: Ohio University Press, 2004.

Engelhardt, George W. *Buffalo, New York: The Book of Its Merchants Exchange*. Buffalo, NY: Matthews-Northrup Company, 1897.

Hill, Henry H. *The Municipality of Buffalo: A History*. 4 vols. New York: Lewis Historical Publishing Company, 1923.

Hill, Henry Wayland. *Men of Buffalo*. Chicago: A.N. Marquis & Company, 1902.

A History of the City of Buffalo: Its Men and Institutions. Buffalo, NY: Buffalo Evening News, 1908.

Horton, John Theodore. *History of Northwestern New York*. New York: Lewis Historical Publishing Company, 1947.

Larned, J.N. *History of Buffalo*. 2 vols. New York: Progress of the Empire State Company, 1911.

Matthews, G.E. *The Men of New York: A Collection of Biographies and Portraits of Citizens of the Empire State Prominent in Business, Professional, Social, and Political Life During the Last Decade of the Nineteenth Century*. 2 vols. Buffalo, NY: G.E. Matthews & Company, 1898.

McGarry, Edmund D. *University of Buffalo Studies in Business*. 2 vols. Buffalo, NY: Bureau of Business and Social Research, 1930.

Miller, Jeffrey. *Buffalo's Forgotten Champions*. N.p.: Xlibris Corporation, 2004.

Mueller, Jacob E. *Buffalo and Its German Community Illustrated*. Buffalo, NY: German-American Historical and Biographical Society, 1912.

Plunkett-Powell, Karen. *Remembering Woolworth's*. New York: St. Martin's Press, 2001.

Retail Trade in the Buffalo Area, Based on the 1948 U.S. Census of Business. Buffalo, NY: Buffalo Census Committee, 1952.

Rizzo, Michael F. *Through the Mayors' Eyes*. Buffalo, NY: Lulu Press, 2005.

Ross, Peter. *The Scot in America*. New York: Raeburn Book Company, 1896.

Shaw, Robert. *History of the Comstock Patent Medicine Business and Dr. Morse's Indian Root Pills*. Project Gutenberg E-Book, September 8, 2004. http://gutenberg.mirrors. tds.net/pub/gutenberg.org/1/3/3/9/13397/13397-h/13397-h.htm.

Smith, H. Perry. *History of the City of Buffalo and Erie County*. 2 vols. Syracuse, NY: D. Mason & Company, 1884.

Thomas, Bernice L. *America's 5 & 10 Cent Stores: The Kress Legacy*. New York: John Wiley & Sons Inc., 1997.

Whitaker, Jan. *Service and Style*. New York: St. Martin's Press, 2006.

Winkler, John K. *Five and Ten: the Fabulous Life of F.W. Woolworth*. New York: Bantam Books, 1957.

Newspapers

Buffalo Daily Courier. November 1, 1842–June 13, 1926.

Buffalo Evening News/Buffalo News. April 11, 1881–present.

Buffalo Express. January 2, 1846–June 13, 1926.

Buffalo Illustrated Express. January 2, 1846–June 13, 1926.

Buffalo Times. December 13, 1883–July 30, 1939.

Courier-Express. June 14, 1926–September 19, 1982.

New York Times. May 1, 1909–present.

Niagara Falls Gazette. July 29, 1926.

MISCELLANEOUS RESOURCES

AM&A's: Adam, Meldrum & Anderson Co, 100 Years, 1867–1967. Buffalo, NY: AM&A's, 1967. Company booklet.

Archivaria. "Buffalo and Its German Community." http://www.archivaria.com/BusDbios/BusDbios25.html.

———. "The Magnificent Success of a Firm." http://www.archivaria.com/BFP/BFP2.4.1902.html.

Bills Backers United. "History of Pro Football in Western New York." http://www.billsbackers.com/BEGINNINGS.htm.

Buffalo and Erie County Historical Society. *Niagara Frontier*, 1953–83.

Buffalo and Erie County Public Library. *Industry in Buffalo.* Buffalo, NY: self-published, n.d.

———. *Local Biographies Scrapbook.* Buffalo, NY: self-published, n.d.

Buffalo and Erie County Public Library vertical files, Buffalo, New York.

Buffalo Architecture and History. "John D. Larkin and the Larkin Company." http://www.buffaloah.com/h/jw/larkin.html.

Buffalo Business Magazine. Publications of the Buffalo Chamber of Commerce, 1934–74.

Buffalo City Directory. 1828–present, Buffalo and Erie County Public Library.

Buffalo Historical Society. *Publications of the Buffalo Historical Society.* 34 vols. Buffalo, NY: self-published, 1879–1959.

Buffalo Saturday Night. Publications of the Buffalo Chamber of Commerce, 1921–23.

Business History Books. "Industries: Business History of Utilities." http://www.businesshistory.com/ind._utilities.php.

Controlled-Demolition, Inc. http://www.controlled-demolition.com.

Cyburgia. http://www.cyburbia.org.

Dead Malls. http://deadmalls.com.

Denton, Cotter & Daniels Pianos & Organs. http://www.dentoncottieranddaniels.com.

Department Store Museum. http://departmentstoremuseum.blogspot.com.

Encyclopedia Titanica. "Mr. Edward Austin Kent." http://www.encyclopedia-titanica.org/titanic-victim/edward-austin-kent.html.

The Great Atlantic & Pacific Tea Company. http://aptea.com.

Greater Buffalo Commission. http://www.greaterbflo.org.

IEEE Global History Network. "Early Electrification of Buffalo: The Beginning of Central Station Service." http://www.ieeeghn.org/wiki/index.php/Early_Electrification_of_Buffalo:_The_Beginning_of_Central_Station_Service.

Internet Archive Wayback Machine. "A&P's History," Great Atlantic & Pacific Tea Company. http://web.archive.org/web/20120422223741/http://www.aptea.com/history_timeline.asp.

———. "King's Department Store." http://web.archive.org/web/20090901120632/http://www.geocities.com/zayre88/R_kings.html.

John Henrich Company Inc. http://johnhenrich.com.

Local History Scrapbook. Ed. Buffalo, NY: Buffalo and Erie County Public Library.

Merriam-Webster Online. http://www.webster.com/dictionary.

MP3 Trusts. "Gene Wisniewski Urban Lucki Jingles." http://mp3trusts.com/index.php?q=wisniewski+gene+lucki+urban+jingles+master+reel+copy+c+1&type=mp3.

National Museum of American History. http://americanhistory.si.edu.

National Park Service. National Register of Historic Places Registration Form, "H.A. Meldrum Company Building." http://www.nps.gov/history/nr/feature/places/pdfs/13000330.pdf.

Old Newark Memories. http://www.oldnewark.com.

Online Archive of California. http://www.oac.cdlib.org.

River Campus Libraries. "Bristol, Cyrenius C." http://www.library.rochester.edu/index.cfm?page=806.

Riverside Men's Shop. "Store History of Riverside Men's Shop." http://www.riversidemens.com/store-history.html.

Tops Friendly Markets. http://www.topsmarkets.com.

Wayne State University Digital Collections. http://dlxs.lib.wayne.edu.

Western New York Heritage Press. http://wnyheritagepress.org.

Wikipedia, the Free Encyclopedia. http://www.wikipedia.org.

Williamson, Samuel H. "Purchasing Power of Money in the United States from 1774 to Present." Measuringworth.com, 2006. http://www.measuringworth.com/calculators/ppowerus.

Woolworths Museum. http:///www.woolworthsmuseum.co.uk.

Index